An Outline of Chinese Literature I

I0591716

Different from previous researches weighted toward historical description and individual writer and work, this book establishes a general analytical system and a multi-angled methodology to examine Chinese literature.

The author Yuan Xingpei is a professor at Peking University, a famous expert on Chinese classic literature. Based on his own appreciation as a reader and years of study, the author expounds on every aspect of Chinese literature: characteristics, time periods, regional nature, categories, allure, transmission, appreciation, etc. It's worth mentioning that the book is written from an individual perspective. The author expresses the depth of his various related impressions of Chinese literature in the book, in the hope that readers can share the emotions. In addition, this book provides readers with many fresh perspectives. For example, it regards poetry being the mainstream, and "upholding goodness," "the spirit of optimism" and "the esthetics of conciseness" as the characteristics of Chinese literature, surpassing the popular academic concepts.

This book will appeal to scholars and students of Chinese literature and comparative literature. People who are interested in Chinese literature and Chinese culture will also benefit from this book.

Yuan Xingpei is a professor in the Department of Chinese Language and Literature, Peking University. His research focuses on Chinese classic literature, especially Chinese poetical art

China Perspectives Series

The *China Perspectives* series focuses on translating and publishing works by leading Chinese scholars writing about both global topics and China-related themes. It covers Humanities & Social Sciences, Education, Media and Psychology, as well as many interdisciplinary themes.

This is the first time any of these books have been published in English for international readers. The series aims to put forward a Chinese perspective, give insights into cutting-edge academic thinking in China, and inspire researchers globally.

For more information, please visit www.routledge.com/series/CPH

Existing titles:

Beyond the Iron House
Lu Xun and the Modern Chinese Literary Field
Sun Saiyin

Forthcoming titles:

Literature and Literary Criticism in Contemporary China
Zhang Jiong

Literature and Literary Theory in Contemporary China
Zhang Jiong

An Outline of Chinese Literature I
Yuan Xingpei

An Outline of Chinese Literature II
Yuan Xingpei

Seven Lectures on Wang Guowei's Renjian Cihua
Florence Chia-Ying Yeh

An Outline of Chinese Literature I

Yuan Xingpei
Translated by Paul White

Routledge
Taylor & Francis Group

LONDON AND NEW YORK

First published 2018
by Routledge

2 Park Square, Milton Park, Abingdon, Oxfordshire OX14 4RN
52 Vanderbilt Avenue, New York, NY 10017

Routledge is an imprint of the Taylor & Francis Group, an informa business

First issued in paperback 2020

British Library Cataloguing-in-Publication Data
A catalogue record for this book is available from the British Library

Library of Congress Cataloging-in-Publication Data
A catalog record for this book has been requested

ISBN: 978-1-138-21940-3 (hbk)
ISBN: 978-0-367-52894-2 (pbk)

Typeset in Times New Roman
by Apex CoVantage, LLC

Contents

Foreword to the Chinese edition

In September 1987 I was invited by Professor Nagashima of Japan's Aichi University to teach an outline course in Chinese literature. On my way back home via Hong Kong personages in Hong Kong's publishing circles, on seeing my lecture notes, decided that they deserved to be published, and so they were sent to the printer. Due to their kind care, this small volume came to be presented to the readers.

Although this book was written for foreigners who wish to study Chinese literature, the requirements of the Chinese reader have also been fully taken into account. For a long time our research into Chinese literature has been weighted toward historical description and discussions of individual writers and works, and too little attention has been paid to many other aspects of the subject as well as to an overall analysis. The style of writing literary history has hardened into a rigid model – one it is not easy to break away from. In these circumstances, it is hoped that this attempt to expound on Chinese literature using the method of an outline can provide readers with fresh perspectives and awaken in them a deeper interest in the subject.

In the course of compiling this book I have consulted a wide range of authorities and studies and duly noted where I am indebted to them. Some have pointed me in the direction of deeper consideration, and some have furnished me with clues for my research. Although I am not able to cite them one by one, let me take this opportunity to thank them all here. I may mention for special thanks for their assistance Mr. Guo Shaoyu, author of *A History of Chinese Literary Criticism*; Mr. Chu Binjie, author of *An Introduction to Ancient Chinese Inscriptions* and Mr. Qi Zhiping, author of *A Brief Account of Tang and Song Poetry*. Special thanks also go to Meng Erdong and Ma Zili, who helped me with the proofreading of the whole text. Due to the author's limited scholarship, there are bound to be omissions and errors, and he hopes that the readers will bring them to his attention.

Finally, my heartfelt thanks go out to Aichi University and Professor Nagashima. If it had not been for their kind invitation and "assignment" perhaps this book would never have been written.

Yuan Xingpei
December 1987

Preface to the Chinese edition

The word "literature" appeared in China even before the time of the Qin Dynasty (221–206 BC). But it had a different connotation from what we mean by "literature" today. In the Confucian classic known as the *Analects* we find the disciples of Confucius divided into four categories of specialty:

> Virtuous conduct: Yan Yuan, Min Ziqian, Ran Boniu and Zhong Gong.
> Eloquence: Zai Wo and Zi Gong.
> Politics: Ran You and Ji Lu.
> Literature: Zi You and Zi Xia.[1]

Xing Bing, in his *The Analects Annotated*, defines the two characters which make up the Chinese word "literature" as follows: "learned in written works."[2] And Yang Xiong, in his *Discourses on Methods * Gentleman*, says, "Zi You and Zi Xia were accomplished at letters."[3] In the *History of the Han Dynasty * Biography of Dong Zhongshu*, it says, "There was a strict ban on literature, and no one could walk around with books under his arm."[4] The word "literature" here originally meant ancient documents. Yang Bojun backs this interpretation in his *The Analects Explained and Annotated* by saying, "Steeped in ancient documents were Zi You and Zi Xia."[5]

The Han Dynasty (206 BC–220 AD) saw a change in the understanding of the word "literature," when it came to mean "learning" in general. As the *Records of the Historian * Chronicle of Li Wu* notes: "In order to spread the Confucian teachings, he summoned the worthy Zhao Wan and Wang Zang and made them senior ministers on account of their learning. And to discuss ancient matters a special hall was set up in the south of the city where the feudal lords who were attending the court could gather."[6]

Zhao Wan and Wang Zang were leading Confucian scholars. The *Records of the Historian * Biographies of Confucian Scholars* says: "The emperor dispatched famous Confucianists in high positions like Zhao Wan and Wang Zang to the provinces and summoned to his court upright and worthy men, scholars renowned for their learning."[7]

By comparing these two passages we can clearly see that "literature" at this time meant Confucian learning. Zhao Wan and Wang Zang were scholars, but not in the modern sense. In the *Records of the Historian * Preface by Sima Qian*, it says: "And so the Han Dynasty flourished. Xiao He put the laws in order. Han Xin expounded on the military disciplines. Zhang Cang enacted the rules and regulations. Shusun Tong arranged the rites and ceremonies. And so it was that literature advanced in elegance, the *Book of Odes* and the *Book of Documents* were issued in several printings."[8]

Here we can see that the law, military discipline, rules and regulations and rites and ceremonies were all included under the heading of "literature."

It is worth noticing that in Han times, besides "wenxue" the word "wenzhang" was also used. The latter denoted non-scholastic writing. In the *History of the Han Dynasty * Eulogy to Gongsun Hong, Bu Shi and Er Kuan*, it says: "The Han Dynasty had a plethora of talented men. In the field of general erudition outstanding were Gongsun Hong, Dong Zhongshu and Er Kuan . . . and in the field of non-scholastic writing, Sima Qian and Sima Xiangru."[9]

Celebrated for their non-scholastic writings were Liu Xiang and Wang Bao . . . who advocated filial piety and the inheritance of tradition.[10]

"Wenzhang" covered such genres as *cifu* (mixed prose and poetry) and historical accounts, in other words styles of writing displaying elegant wording. As for the difference between "wenxue" and "wenzhang," the clearest definition may be in the words of Xiahou Hui in the *Annals of the Three Kingdoms*: "Xiahou Hui, in an encouraging tone, said, 'A *wenxue* scholar takes care to advance his theme using elaborate detail, while a *wenzhang* scholar takes pride in the close integration of his words.'"[11]

Moreover, the people of Han times took great care over the meaning of words and stressed their composition and use. This is different from what we today call "literature."

Advancing a little from the difference between "wenxue" and "wenzhang" in the Han Dynasty, during the Southern Dynasties (420–589) there emerged a difference between "wen" (writing) and "bi" (writing brush). In the *History of the Southern Dynasties * Biography of Yan Yan*, we find: "The emperor once asked Yan Zi about the ability needed by his officials." Yan Zi replied, 'The quality of his writing is the measure of an official's literary attainment.'"[12]

Liu Xie says in his *Carving a Dragon with a Literary Heart * Chronological Sequence*: "Yu used his writing to endear people to him; Wen used literature to make his own thoughts more generous."[13] In his *Chapter on the Arts*, the same author says, "It is often said that there is literature and there is writing: The latter is not full of pleasing sounds; the former is."[14]

Using the presence or absence of pleasing sounds as the criterion for distinguishing "literature" from "writing" was a concept which sprang up early in history. Xiao Yi, Emperor Yuan (reign: 552–555) of Liang, in his *The Golden Tower * Eternal Words*, says, "In ancient times there were two ways of scholarship; nowadays there are four."[15]

The two ways of "scholarship" of ancient times he is referring to are the "literature" and "writings" of the Han Dynasty; the four ways of "scholarship" of his own day are "Confucian studies" and "learning," into which "Wenxue" was divided, and "literature" and "writings," into which "Wenzhang" was divided. In the *Chapter on Bequeathing Writings to Posterity* there is a further elaboration on the difference between "literature" and "writings":

> Qu Yuan, Song Yu, Mei Cheng, Chang Qing and their ilk confined themselves to writing *cifu*, which they called literature. . . . As for the works of people like Yan Zuan, whose poetry is awkward, and Bo Song, whose talent lay in composing memorials to the throne, they come under the general heading of "bi" or "writings." The chanting of ballads and long-drawn-out dirges were included in the category of "literature." . . . As for "writings," at the very least they would be called incomplete, and at the very most meaningless. They were regarded as mere clever exercises in composition. As for literary works, they had to be elaborate and embroidered, with high-flown phrases and sentiments.[16]

Xiao Yi's demarcation between "wen" and "bi" was not one simply between the presence and absence of pleasing sounds. He in fact recognized that the characteristic of "wen" was its ability to stir the emotions and thereby rouse men to action. "Wen" also had the value of providing enjoyment through its emphasis on the beauty of its diction (rhythm and flourishes, etc.). "Bi" was the writing style used to frame memorials to the throne and suchlike. As Zhang Binglin said, "'Wen' is used for poetical and *fu* (mixed poetry and prose) works; 'bi' for official documents. That was what they used to say in those days."[17] The "cleverness" in "bi" writings was restricted to the technique of composition and could not be compared to the qualities of "wen."

Xiao Yi's emphasis on the two special characteristics of emotion and diction in "wen" are close to what we today would call "literature." However, the influence of his *The Golden Tower* was not great; the biggest influence on the theory of literary style in China was exerted by two works which appeared at different times: *Carving a Dragon with a Literary Heart* and *Selected Works of Literature.* These two works did not make clear distinction between "wen" and "bi." In the category of "wen" they included the forms of applied writing such as edicts, lyrics, summonses and didactics. This situation lasted down to the Qing Dynasty (1644–1911) with the appearance of *A Compilation of Classical Prose* by Yao Nai, an antiquarian of the Tongcheng school. This work contains prose writings in the ancient style dating from the Warring States Period (475–221 BC) to the Qing Dynasty, and includes applied genres.

In traditional bibliographies too the scope of literature is not clear. Xun Xu of the Western Jin Dynasty (265–317) divided writings into four categories which he labeled A, B, C and D. Li Chong of the Eastern Jin Dynasty (317–420) combined Xun Xu's B and C categories and divided writings into classics, histories, philosophy and anthologies. But what the bibliographers called anthologies were equivalent to neither what Xiao Yi called collections of "wen" nor what are today called anthologies of literary works. On the one hand, the first included many applied writing genres, some of which could be classified as literature and some of which could not. It is necessary to examine their concrete circumstances before deciding. On the other hand, novels and opera scripts, which today would be regarded as indispensable parts of anthologies of literature, are not included in the ancient collections. Novels written in classical Chinese were included under the heading of history or philosophy. Novels written in colloquial language and opera scripts were basically ignored by the bibliographers.

To sum up: In ancient China there was no strict division between literary and non-literary writing. In fact, there was no definite concept of pure literature as such. What was called literature in the old days included, on the one hand, genres which we nowadays would not consider as belonging to the category of literature at all, and on the other, excluded genres which we would include as literature. Therefore, when we embark on a study of Chinese literature we must not only take into account modern ideas of literature but also the more diverse concept of literature that is traditional in China. Based on this principle, this book broadly discusses poetry (including its *fu*, *ci* and *qu* subgenres), the novel and discursive writing.

Notes

1 *Commentary on the Thirteen Classics*, World Bookstore photocopy of the Ruan woodblock print, P. 2498
2 *Commentary on the Thirteen Classics*, World Bookstore photocopy of the Ruan woodblock print, P. 2498
3 *Collected Works of the Philosophers*, Vol. 7, Shanghai Bookstore, 1991, P. 39
4 Ban Gu [Han Dynasty]: *History of the Han Dynasty*, Vol. 56, Zhonghua Book Company, 1962, P. 2504
5 Yang Bojun: *The Analects Explained and Annotated*, Zhonghua Book Company, 1980, P. 110
6 Sima Qian [Han Dynasty]: *Records of the Historian*, Vol. 12, Zhonghua Book Company, 1959, P. 452
7 Sima Qian [Han Dynasty]: *Records of the Historian*, Vol. 121, Zhonghua Book Company, 1959, P. 3118
8 Sima Qian [Han Dynasty]: *Records of the Historian*, Vol. 130, Zhonghua Book Company, 1959, P. 3319
9 Ban Gu [Han Dynasty]: *History of the Han Dynasty*, Vol. 58, Zhonghua Book Company, 1962, P. 2634
10 Ban Gu [Han Dynasty]: *History of the Han Dynasty*, Vol. 58, Zhonghua Book Company, 1962, P. 2634
11 Chen Shou [Jin Dynasty]: *Annals of the Three Kingdoms*, Vol. 21, *Biography of Liu Shao*, Zhonghua Book Company, 1963, P. 619
12 Li Yanshou [Tang Dynasty]: *History of the Southern Dynasties*, Vol. 34, Zhonghua Book Company, 1975, P. 879
13 Fan Wenlan: *Carving a Dragon With a Literary Heart Annotated*, Vol. 9, People's Literature Publishing House, 1978, P. 674
14 Fan Wenlan: *Carving a Dragon With a Literary Heart Annotated*, Vol. 9, People's Literature Publishing House, 1978, P. 655
15 Xiao Yi [The Liang Court of the Southern Dynasties]: *The Golden Tower * Eternal Words*, Vol. 4, *Collected Works From Lack of Knowledge Studio*, Vol. 9, woodblock print, sixth year (1826) of the Daoguang reign period of the Qing Dynasty
16 Xiao Yi [The Liang Court of the Southern Dynasties]: *The Golden Tower * Eternal Words*, Vol. 4, *Collected Works From Lack of Knowledge Studio*, Vol. 9, woodblock print, sixth year (1826) of the Daoguang reign period of the Qing Dynasty
17 Zhang Binglin: *Discussing China's Culture * Literary Symposium*, Original Text with Notes, Shanghai Ancient Works Propagation Publishing House, P. 41

Part I

The characteristics of Chinese literature

The study of the characteristics of Chinese literature has an inseparable bond with the overall characteristics of Chinese culture, and necessitates probing deeply into the nature of literature itself. As for the overall characteristics of Chinese culture, the author's *Reflections on the Theory of Chinese Literature* summarizes the following five aspects as the contents of Chinese ideological civilization: the theory of Yin and Yang, spiritual culture, respect for virtue and esteem for society, clinging to the middle ground and collective thinking.[1]

To investigate the characteristics of Chinese literature it is necessary to pay attention to the special nature of the Chinese language and its writing system, and their influence on Chinese literature. For example: Chinese is not an inflectional language, which means that it does not have a rigid system of changes of form to express changes in meaning. It does not have limitations of time, number, sex or case. The structure of a Chinese sentence relies more on sense than form. Standard Chinese differentiates between four tones. The writing system is not phonetic; each character represents one syllable, and many characters are actually pictographs. It is because the Chinese language and writing system have these characteristics that Chinese the study of Chinese literature can take into account antithetical balance and combinations of tones, and their parallel usage in modern poetry. It is because the Chinese language has these characteristics that words and phrases and images can be linked in a lively way, prepositions and conjunctions can be omitted, and images can be directly assembled in a lively presentation of time and space, subject and object. This gives a spirited effect to literary works, leaving broad scope for the reader's imagination. This is especially suited to the expression of poetic artistry.[2]

The characteristics of Chinese literature discussed in this section naturally have much in common with the characteristics of Chinese culture, language and writing. But these two topics are too broad to be dealt with as a whole and will be touched upon in their proper places. This section will focus on promoting discussion and clarification of the characteristics of Chinese literature itself, and will, of course, be helpful for an understanding of the overall characteristics of Chinese literature.

1 Poetry is the mainstream

The main current of the long river of Chinese literature is formed of poetry and ballads. This is discussed from five aspects below:

1. The origin of Chinese poetry and ballads is lost in the mists of time. The earliest collection of poems and ballads in China is the *Book of Odes*, compiled between the 11th and sixth centuries BC, or some 3,000 years ago. By comparison, Homer's *Iliad* and *Odyssey* are probably products of the ninth to eighth centuries BC. The *Ramayana* of ancient India is a product of the third to second centuries BC, and the epic *Mahabharata* was produced in ancient India after the beginning of the first century BC. All these works were later than China's *Book of Odes*.

Following the *Book of Odes*, many fine poets and fine poetic works appeared. In fact, the excellent tradition of poems and ballads in China has never been interrupted. Two high points of China's history of poetry and balladeering came in the Tang (618–907) and Song (960–1279) Dynasties. The poetic stage in those years can be aptly described as a "star-studded autumn sky,"[3] providing endless beauty. The *Complete Tang Poems*, compiled in the Kangxi reign period (1662–1723) of the Qing Dynasty, contains 48,900 works by 2,200 poets. The *Complete Song Ci Poems*, compiled by the modern scholar Tang Guizhang, contains 19,900 works by 1,330 poets. These collections do not exhaust the Tang and Song poetic repertoire by any means, but they give us some idea of how flourishing it was. In fact, the Tang and Song poetic works are a source of great pride to the Chinese people.

Compared to the lengthy tradition of poems and ballads, the novel and the drama in China were tardy bloomers. They joined the long river of literature quite late. In fact, it was not until the Tang Dynasty, in the eighth century, that the novel appeared, in the form of *chuan qi*, or short stories written in classical language. The drama slowly came to maturity in the period of the Song and Jin (1115–1234) Dynasties, and reached its full flowering in the Yuan Dynasty, in the 13th century, some 1,800 years after the Greek tragicomedy and over 2,000 years after the *Book of Odes*.

Lyricism is the mainstay of the Chinese poetry and ballad genre. Epic was developed in ancient Greece and India. There were no long epics in the literature of ancient China, which was written in Chinese characters; or at least no tradition of such long epics has been handed down to us.[4] The poems "The Birth of Ancestors" and "Everlasting" in the *Book of Odes* indeed have the flavor of national epics, but they are short and concise and do not have the grandeur of the epic. Not only does Chinese literature lack the epic genre, even long narrative poems are rare. "The Peacock Flies Southeast," written at the end of the Han Dynasty, and the "The Song of Mulan," which dates from the Northern Dynasties (386–581), are two famous narrative poems of the folk ballad genre. However, they are not long, and their plots are crudely drawn and not fully developed. The works of the Tang poets Du Fu and Bai Juyi and the Qing Dynasty poet Wu Weiye, titled, "Three Officials," Three Partings," "The Long Lament," "Song of the Lute" and "Rondel," are deeply imbued with lyricism, but the number of such poems is few. The nature of Chinese poetry and ballads can be expressed as "poetic aspiration"[5] or "poetic expression of destiny."[6] The most common subjects of Chinese poems and ballads are expression of one's innermost feelings and life course, allegorical attacks on the times, praise of the natural scenery, border garrison duty, the wanderer longing for his wife, love and marriage and exchanges of gifts between friends. All these tend to emphasize feelings and aspirations, with little room left for narrative. If we say that poems and ballads are the mainstream of Chinese literature, then lyric poetry is the mainstream of this mainstream, and therefore lyricism itself naturally occupies an important place in Chinese literature.

2. The instructive function of poetry, to which a lot of attention has always been paid in China, is sometimes called the theory of "poetic instruction." In the *Book of Rites * Explanation of the Classics* we find, "Confucius said, 'Upon entering another state, one can easily grasp the level of its education. If its people are gentle and honest one can know that they have been taught the *Book of Odes*.'" His meaning was that by observing a state's customs one can know how educated its people are. If they are gentle and honest, then this is because of the instructional function of poetry. It also means that poetry can imbue a person with the gentle and honest nature of a person of humanity. Confucius reminded his disciples of the importance of studying the *Book of Odes* in the following passage from the *Analects * Yang Huo*: "Confucius said, 'My children, why do you not study the *Book of Odes*? The *Odes* serve to stimulate the mind. They may be used for purposes of self-contemplation. They teach the art of sociability. They show how to regulate feelings of resentment. From them you learn the more immediate duty of serving one's father, and the remoter one of serving one's prince. From them we become largely acquainted with the names of birds, beasts, and plants.'"[7] This passage touches on various functions of poetry – the emotional, cognitive and social and psychological easing – as well as its various uses in home and government life. In the *Analects * Ji Shi*, we read, "He [Confucius] was standing alone once, when I [Kong Li, Confucius' son] passed below the hall with hasty steps. He said to me: 'Have you learned the *Odes*?' On my replying 'Not yet,' he added, 'If you do not learn the *Odes*, you will not be fit to converse with.' I retired and studied the *Odes*."[8] In this instruction to his son, Confucius stresses that a person who has not studied the *Book of Odes* is not fit to converse with, and, moreover, will never move in the upper echelons of society. Here, Confucius' emphasis on the function of poetry in teaching the art of rhetoric is connected with the custom during the Spring and Autumn Period (770–476 BC), covering the period when

Confucius lived, of reciting poetry on diplomatic occasions to hint at one's true meaning.

3. The recital of poetry on diplomatic occasions was done to express or hint at one's meaning when the use of blunt language would have seemed too challenging, or "undiplomatic." And so we could call this for the time being "poetic and ballad diplomacy." An instance can be found in the *Zuo Zhuan * 13th year of Duke Wen of Lu*: Following the severing of the ruler of the State of Zheng's allegiance to the State of Jin and his paying homage to the king of Chu, the Zheng ruler had second thoughts and wanted to restore his old alliance with Jin. It happened at that time that Duke Wen of Lu had just returned from a visit to Jin. The ruler of Zheng arranged a meeting with him at which he asked Duke Wen to intercede for him with Jin. The exchanges between the two sides were expressed through the medium of poetry. Again, in the *Zuo Zhuan * 23rd year of Duke Xi of Lu* we find Duke Wen of Jin and Duke Mu of Qin exchanging snatches of verse:

> Another day Duke Mu invited Chong Er to a banquet. Hu Yan said to Chong Er: "I am not as accomplished in literary studies as Zhao Cui; let him accompany you."
>
> At the feast, Chong Er recited the poem "River Water," to indicate that after he returned to the State of Jin he would follow the wishes of the ruler of Qin.
>
> Duke Mu recited "Six Months" [from the *Book of Odes*] to express his hope that Chong Er would prove to be a faithful vassal of the king of Zhou when he recovered the throne of Jin.
>
> Zhao Cui exclaimed, "Crown Prince Chong Er has fittingly expressed his appreciation for Duke Mu's kindness!"
>
> Chong Er descended from the dais upon which he sat to kowtow to Duke Mu, while the latter descended one step to acknowledge the courtesy. Thereupon, Zhao Cui said, "Sire, Crown Prince Chong Er will never dare to refuse to carry out your command to serve the House of Zhou faithfully."

This anecdote tells how Chong Er, a prince of the State of Jin, was entertained at a banquet by Duke Mu of Qin as he passed through the latter state during his exile. Chong Er and Duke Mu exchanged opinions by means of reciting poetry. In "River Water," Chong Er used the image of the sea to refer to his host's court, and the river to refer to himself. In this way, he hints at his subordinate attitude toward the State of Qin. Duke Mu recites "Six Months" from the *Book of Odes * Minor Court Hymns*, which describes how Yi Jifu assists his ruler, King Xuan of Zhou, on a military expedition. He hinted that upon his return to power in his native state [Jin], Chong Er would prove a staunch supporter of the House of Zhou. In this way, Duke Mu expressed his trust in and support for Chong Er. And so Zhao Cui, who had accompanied Chong Er to the banquet, lost no time reminding the duke of Chong Er's gratitude, making it quite clear that he understood and approved of the meaning of Duke Mu's choice of poem. But it seems regrettable that this type of "poetic diplomacy" is found only in ancient China.

4. The importance of poetry can also be shown by the fact that the ability to compose poetry was a necessary condition for entry to an official career during the Tang Dynasty. During that period a "scholar-gentleman" was a person who could write poetry in the *shi* and *fu* styles then in vogue. According to research done by Mr. Fu Xuanzong, "It was in the eighth century that *shi* and *fu* poetry were included in the requirements for the *jinshi* degree [the highest level of the civil service examination], and in the Tianbao reign period (742–756) of Tang Emperor Xuanzong the ability to write poetry in these styles became a fixed requirement for a 'scholar-gentleman.'"[9] The earliest work in the *Complete Tang Poems* is by Chen Xilie (?–757), who lived in the early years of the reign of Emperor Xuanzong. It appears under the heading of "Attempts." Titled, "Provincial Test: Amidst the Opening and Unfolding of White Clouds," it reads,

> Mount Tai's peak has soared for a thousand years,
> The clouds rise on the King of Han's demise.
> They do not make the peaks exotic,
> but prefer to shape the wondrous rocks.
> Although the autumn rain is timely,
> it is difficult to encounter a sage.
> Slowly the clouds cover the sky,
> Loath to part, the phantom shapes flicker.
> The pure light does not linger,
> The spiritual gift follows the dragon.
> How can I study what the heart itself does not reach?
> When east and west both obey their calling?[10]

The more famous poem is Qian Qi's "Provincial Test: The Spirit of the Xiang River Plays a Zither," which reads,

> Good at playing the *Yunhe* zither, I often hear,
> Is the spirit of Dizi, King Shun's beloved wife.
> The river god Pingyi dances alone to the tune,
> But I, a visitor from afar, find it too saddening.
> So much so it can even move metal and stone,
> Its resonance reaching into the farthest realm.
> It has aroused King Shun reposing on Mount Cangwu,
> And caused bitter *Baizhi* plants to emit their fragrance.
> The music streams to the Xiang River like flowing water,
> And sweeps over the vast Dongting Lake like rueful wind.
> Now that the zither's stopped, its player is still invisible,
> Leaving a few mountains standing in verdant tranquility.[11]

There are not many elegant poems in the "Attempts" style. This is a fact. But it is also true that they undoubtedly helped to raise the level of the writing of poetry and ballads by encouraging "scholar-gentlemen" to study and practice poetic composition.

5. Poetry and ballads had an important influence on not only other genres of literature but also on all other aspects of art in China. Their impact on expository writing is particularly obvious; in fact, prose writing especially was a result of the influence of poetry and ballads. Broadly speaking, prose writing emerged in the Wei and Jin Dynasties (220–420), and, along with the birth of a new type of versification in the Southern Dynasties, reached its maturity and flourished. All types of writing in this period – from narrative and lyric prose to discussions, edicts, memorials and notices of publication – used the form of prose writing. Liu Xie's *Carving a Dragon with a Literary Heart*, which expounds on literary theory, is written in this style. The antithetic technique, phonetic rules and sentence balance of prose writing in this period all show clearly the artistic traits of the China's poetry and ballad tradition.

Both the Chinese novel and drama have the tendency to get close to poetry and ballad, or, one could say, a sort of tendency toward the poetic. Looking at the history of the development of the novel, we find that the ancient novel, i.e., that which emerged before the Tang Dynasty, was not much more than a bald narrative or "street gossip," and could hardly be regarded as a self-conscious literary creation. It was during the Tang Dynasty, when poetry and ballads throve to a high degree, that the novel absorbed poetic nourishment and grew to be a literary work which clearly delineated human images and described well-rounded plots. The *chuanqi* [strange tales] genre of short story of the Tang Dynasty owes much of the origin and development of its descriptive elegance, soaring imagination, ornate vocabulary and freshness of style to the influence of Tang poetry. In fact, many of the authors of such short stories were poets themselves, who looked at life through a poet's eyes and used the novel form to express lyrical feelings, reaching a level in this regard that their predecessors had failed to reach. Representative *chuanqi* short stories such as *The Story of the Long Lament*, *The Story of Li Wa*, *The Story of Yingying*, *The Story of Liu Yi* and *The Story of Huo Xiaoyu* are all permeated with a poetic aroma.

The vernacular novels of the Song and Yuan (1206–1368) Dynasties have an inseparable bond with the poetic and ballad tradition. During the Song Dynasty there were four schools of the vernacular storytelling art form. Three of them – the novel, the *shuojing* and the *hesheng* – were combinations of recitation and singing, and the singing parts were in fact poetry. And so the *huaben*, or storytellers' prompt books, are sometimes called *shihua* or *cihua*, meaning prose interspersed with verse. The school which dealt with historical tales generally used prose and eschewed verse in its prompt books, but even there verse sometimes creeps in. In fact, even vernacular novels written by accomplished scholars, such as *A Dream of Red Mansions* and *Flowers in the Mirror* borrow extensively from the art of poetry and the ballad. Drama in China had its origin in folk songs and dances. Some people, with justification, think that Qu Yuan's "Nine Songs" sprang from a primitive song-and-dance drama of ancient China. The flourishing of poetry, ballads and music during the Tang Dynasty laid ample groundwork for the birth of the drama. In addition, the *guzici* and *zhugongdiao* storytelling forms of the Song and Jin (1115–1234), both of which involved prose and verse recitation, led directly to the appearance of the Yuan drama. Among the various elements which went into making up the drama, the libretto occupies an important place. This is because some of the drama plots are quite simple, and they rely on poetic recitation for their effect. And so, Chinese drama is verse drama; divorced from verse, it cannot exist. Of the great dramatists of this period – Guan Hanqing, Wang Shifu, Bai Pu, Ma Zhiyuan, Gao Ming, Tang Xianzu, Hong Sheng and Kong Shangren – which one was not an accomplished poet? Of the famous dramas of this period – *The Injustice Done to Dou E, The Western Chamber, Wutongyu (Rain on the Parasol Tree), Autumn in the Han Palace, The Story of the Lute, The Peony Pavilion, Longevity Hall* and *The Peach Blossom Fan* – which of them is not a fine work of poetry? Take this verse from *The Western Chamber*, for instance: "The azure sky is studded with clouds; the earth is strewn with yellow blossoms. The west wind blows close around, and the northern geese fly south. At daybreak bemused in the frosty forest, overcome with tears of parting." The original is poetry of the highest order in both temperament and rhythm. The fact that poetry seeped into and influenced the novel and drama illustrates the mainstream position that poetry holds in Chinese literature.

The fact that China's poetry and ballad tradition had a far-reaching influence on Chinese art as a whole can be illustrated in the case of painting. Both the schools of freehand painting and meticulous painting for the most part pursued the realm and flavor of poetry. Just as poetry and ballads strove for meaning beyond words, painting strove for meaning beyond shape. The "transcendent," "spiritual" and "superb" works mentioned in the theory of painting can be regarded as works which contain poetic content. The theories of painting and poetry have a lot in common; for instance, the both stress "resonance," "Nature" and "charm."[12] Many painters, such as Wang Wei and Su Shi, were poets as well. And countless paintings were created on the basis of poetic themes, especially those of Tao Yuanming, Wang Wei, Li Bai and Su Shi, who incorporate their poetic subjects into paintings.

From the above five-point analysis of poetry as the mainstream of Chinese literature, we can conclude that it is no exaggeration to say that China is a country of poetry because of the important place that poetry occupies in the country's literature.

Notes

1 From *Reflections on the Theory of Chinese Literature, Research into National Studies*, Vol. 15, Peking University Press, 2005
2 From the author's *Research into the Chinese Art of Poetry and Ballads*, quoted from the Foreword and relevant essays, Peking University Press, 1997
3 Li Bai [Tang Dynasty]: *Ancient Style* No. 1, *Complete Tang Poems*, Vol. 161, Zhonghua Book Company, 1960, P. 1670
4 The most outstanding long epics of China's minority nationalities, such as the *Gesar* of the Tibetans, the *Jangar* of the Mongolians and the *Manas* of the Khirgiz
5 The *Book of Shang * Canon of Yao, Commentary on the Thirteen Classics*, World Bookstore photocopy of the Ruan woodblock print, P. 131
6 Lu Ji [Jin Dynasty]: "Rhapsody on Literature", *Collection of Mr. Lu's Works*, Vol. 1, *Collected Writings of the Four Basic Branches of Literature*

7 *Commentary on the Thirteen Classics*, World Bookstore photocopy of the Ruan wood-block print, P. 2525

8 *Commentary on the Thirteen Classics*, World Bookstore photocopy of the Ruan wood-block print, P. 2522

9 Fu Xuancong: *The Imperial Examination and Literature During the Tang Dynasty*, Shaanxi People's Publishing House, 1986, P. 408

10 According to *A New History of the Tang Dynasty * Biography of Chen Xi*, in the 19th year [731] of the Kaiyuan reign period of Emperor Xuanzong Chen Xi was an Erudite of the Jixian Academy. Before that he was a Secretariat Drafter. So his poetic attempts must have been made before 732. It is said that Zu Yong included an "attempt" in his "Observing the Remnants of the Snow on Mount Zhongnan," produced in 725. See *Records of Tang Poetry*, Vol. 20, Zhonghua Book Company, 1965. The poetic attempts properly had eight characters to a line, and as this poem only has four characters to a line, it is not, strictly speaking, an "attempt." More research is needed

11 *Complete Tang Poems*, Vol. 238, Zhonghua Book Company, 1960, P. 2651

12 See *A Discussion of Chinese Painting*, general editor Wu Mengfu, Anhui Fine Arts Publishing House, 1995; Yuan Xingpei *Natural Charm, Research into National Culture*, Vol. 9, Peking University Press, 2002

2 Upholding goodness

The great German man of letters Wolfgang von Goethe once said, "In thought, action and feelings, the Chinese are almost the same as we are. One would almost jump to the conclusion that they are of the same race as we are, except that they are more romantic, purer and more in tune with virtue."[1] This remark, although it is not confined to literature, nevertheless serves to explain the special nature of Chinese literature. The words "romantic," "pure" and "virtue" which Goethe uses can be generally included in the term "goodness." Both Chinese and Western literature seek a genuine fusion of goodness and beauty. The difference is that Western literature puts "truth" in first place, while Chinese literature puts "goodness" in first place. In the West, the guiding ideology, with the ancient Greek philosophers Plato and Aristotle as the exemplars, has been the theory of formalism. Therefore, Western literature has tended to stress formalism, and regarded "truth" as "beauty." The 19th-century Russian literary critic Chernishevsky came up with the definition that "Beauty is life." In his opinion, art was not simply a "depiction of reality"; the function of art was to repeat life, explain life and pass judgment on the phenomena of life. This could be said to be the acme of the development of formalism and represent the main tradition of Western artistic thought. The traditional attitude in China, with Confucius as its representative, is to put "goodness" as the ultimate object of pursuit. Asked to sum up the 300 poems of the *Book of Odes*, Confucius said, "Have no perverted thoughts."[2] What he meant was that one's mind should never stray from "goodness." This quotation has become an important yardstick for gauging ancient Chinese literature. Confucius said about *The Shao Music*: "They plumb the depths of beauty and they plumb the depths of goodness." About the *Wu* [martial arts]: "They plumb the depths of beauty, but they do not plumb the depths of goodness."[3] In his opinion, it was not enough to simply plumb the depths of beauty; it was only when the utmost beauty was complemented by the utmost goodness that perfection could be reached. This exaltation of goodness was not confined to the Confucianists; it was shared by the Taoists too. The two schools differed only in what each considered to be government of a "good" society: The Confucians regarded governance by benevolence and righteousness as "good," while the Taoists' ideal was a government entirely in accordance with the principles of nature. Laozi (the first sage of Taoism) said, "The highest goodness is like water. Water brings benefits to all, without discrimination."[4] He also said, "Goodness advances, and leaves no traces."[5] When literature is in accord with the principles of nature, then it can be said to be identified with the highest good and the highest beauty.

When the attitude of exaltation of goodness is embodied in literary creation then it becomes a kind of idealism and individual strength. The pursuit of a beautiful ideal and holding fast to a lofty personal character are the most valuable traits of Chinese literature.

All the works of the first great figure in Chinese literary history, Qu Yuan, are imbued with idealism and spiritual and personal beauty. In order to realize his ideal he was "prepared to die in exile" and would "suffer nine deaths without regret." He feared not to stand alone, nor did he fear persecution. He stood against the current of the times, and by doing so he displayed his great personal strength of character. In his collection of poems titled, "Li Sao," Qu Yuan says, "Each life has that in which it delights. I alone make love of self-cultivation my norm."[6] "Love of self-cultivation" includes the idea of exaltation of goodness. On the one hand, it is the political ideal of holding fast to beauty; on the other, it is the fostering in oneself of a fine character. When both these aspects are united in one person they produce an illustrious representative of an ancient Chinese literary figure.

To analyze one step further, the fineness of Qu Yuan's character is above all displayed in his steadfastness. He includes the phrase "alone and unmoving" in his "Song of the Tangerine Bush": "Oh, your young resolution has something different from the rest/Alone and unmoving you stand/How can one not admire you?"[7] This is a reference to the tangerine bush, which the ancients said bore bitter fruit if it were transplanted north of the Huai River.[8] Qu Yuan used it as a metaphor for his attachment to his native land and his sticking sternly to his principles in his political struggles, refusing to drift with the tide. The actions and behavior of Qu Yuan throughout his life are the clearest expressions of his steadfastness. In his day, the power of the Kingdom of Chu was deteriorating constantly under the control of a corrupt aristocracy, and Qu Yuan's suggestions for reform were getting nowhere; not only that, but he was the victim of slander and physical attacks. His situation, in short, was a difficult one indeed. In the poems in his collection titled, "Li Sao" he gives vent to his grievances. Imagining that he has gone to another country to seek an opportunity to put his political program into effect, he imagines that he is hoisted aloft in a chariot drawn by eight dragons. On the chariot is a flag formed of multicolored clouds, which flaps in the breeze. Behind him followed a thousand or more other chariots. On and on they journeyed, until suddenly Qu Yuan looked down from the sky, upon his own hometown. Sorrow overcame his servant, and his steeds suddenly balked at the journey and refused to continue. Qu Yuan too, of course, is reluctant to leave his native land. In the final poem of the "Li Sao" he expresses himself thus: "I wanted to snatch some time for pleasure and amusement/But when I had ascended the splendor of the heavens/I suddenly caught a glimpse below of my old home/The groom's heart was heavy, and the steeds for longing/Arched their heads back, and refused to go on./Enough! There are no true men in the state/No one to understand me/Why should I cleave to the place of my birth?/Since none is worthy to work with in making good government/I will go and join Peng Xian in the place where he abides."[9] Here Qu Yuan states that he would rather follow the example of the ancient worthy Peng Xian in taking his own life than leave the land of his birth.

How can one be alone and unmoving? Qu Yuan had two principles: One was "not seeking," and the other was "awake to this world's ways." In the "Song of the Tangerine Bush" he says, "Oh, your young resolution has something different from the rest/Alone and unmoving you stand/How can one not admire you?/Deep-rooted, hard to shift/Truly you have no peer/Awake to this world's ways, alone you stand/unyielding against the vulgar tide." First, he stresses "not seeking," for all those who drift with the current are seeking something. Only when one does not seek private advantage can one become unyielding and unmoved by others, and preserve one's independent, dauntless nature. The other principle, that of "awake to this world's ways," means having a constantly clear head and being keenly aware of right and wrong at all times. Then and only then can one preserve one's independence and not drift with the current.

Another aspect of the fineness of Qu Yuan's character was his spirit of exploration both of the high and the low. His "Asking Heaven" contains over 170 topics of inquiry, covering astronomy, geography, history, government and many others. "Asking Heaven" is a record of Qu Yuan's lofty philosophical probing for the laws of the universe and society. The verses in Qu Yuan's representative work, "Li Sao," revolve round two major questions: What is the way of salvation for the Kingdom of Chu and what is the way of salvation for the poet himself? They are like the main melody in a musical tune, coming round and round again, and seeking a rational answer to the question: What am I looking for? "The road goes on and on, and I seek high and low." This verse encapsulates a search that has been pursued down the ages.

Li Bai, also known as Li Bo, a great poet of the Tang Dynasty, left a brilliant page in the history of Chinese literature with his idealistic poems and songs. We can glimpse the loftiness of his lyrical idealism in his description of the roc:

> Once a gust of strong wind comes up,
> A roc can soar to the zenith of the sky.
> Should the wind stop to bring it down,
> It could still jolt the waters of the sea.
> Heroic utterances I make now and then;
> Sneering at me are but common folks.
> Even Confucius respected the young;
> You can't snub me because of my age![10]

He often compared himself to Lu Zhonglian, Fan Li, Le Yi, Zhu Hai, Hou Ying and Xie An. He hoped that he too could be like them, relying on his own knowledge and courage to benefit and comfort the people, and make some outstanding achievement. "Leaning on my sword/Sleepless at night/I chant aloud/For my distant country/I vow to fight."[11] "In death, fragrance of courage persists/Making me a worthy hero of this world."[12] What a heroic aspiration Li Bai cherished! Being the loftiest of his time in character, Li Bai displayed at the same time his desire to pursue beautiful ideals, his eagerness to maintain an independent personality, and his determination to advocate conduct marked by benevolence. He said, "Proudly aloof and honestly upright by nature/A pine can't covet favor like a gaudy peach."[13] "I'd rather die honest and frank in the grass/Than survive humiliated in a cage of gold."[14] He refused to bow and scrape to those with wealth and power, and considered it shameful to be included in the ranks of flunkeys. He had the sort of character which attracts the readers of his poems.

The Song Dynasty poet Lu You has an extremely moving effect on people with the exalted ideals he expresses in his works. He had a heroic style and expressed his ideals in a constantly lyrical manner: With the courage to "wipe out the remaining enemies with a single blow," Lu You constantly stressed his ambitions:

> To win honor on faraway frontiers is my long-cherished desire.
> With my dagger-axe, I'll charge the enemy for my empire.
> A soldier must fight to the end of his life.
> It's shameful to remain in the bosom of my family.[15]
> Lying stiff and cold in a lonely village, I'm not pitying myself.
> I'm thinking of defending the Luntai frontier instead.
> Hearing a sputtering rainstorm late at night,
> I dream of armored horses galloping on frozen rivers.[16]
> Upon dreaming of the Songting Pass's recapture at night,
> I jolted awake and, stroking my pillow, I cried out loud.[17]

Lu You's lofty spirit is amply expressed in these poems brimming with passionate patriotism.

Pu Songling, in his *Strange Tales from a Chinese Studio*, describes with the greatest fervor a batch of kind-hearted people who dare to combat the forces of evil and take the initiative in helping others to overcome difficulties. In addition, untrammelled by feudal morality, they engage freely in love and marriage. In his characterizations of these people, Pu Songling projects his own progressive ideals and the aspirations of ordinary people for a beautiful life. Some of his ideal people appear in the form of witches and fox spirits. From the pen of Pu Songling many of his fox spirits turn out to be models of goodness, courage and fighting verve. Representatives of these are "Red Jade," "Third Sister Feng," "Crow Head," "Fourteenth Sister Xin," "Jiaona" and "Little Cui." Ying Ning, who was born of a fox spirit, is a naturally unaffected little girl. Unrestrained by anything, honest and straightforward, she is full of refreshing liveliness. Wherever she goes, she smiles and laughs without restraint. She climbs to the tops of trees, where she "laughs until she nearly falls down." Pu Songling pours all his disdain for feudal ethics into this girl. He calls her "my Ying Ning." It is quite obvious that she is the author's model of an ideal young woman. The fox fairy Little Cui is an even more convention-defying character, completely natural and full of life. She paints her husband's face to make him look like a devil, and even dresses him up to look like an emperor. There is no jest she will not get up to. Pu Songling has boundless admiration for her too. All these examples show that Pu Songling's "exaltation of goodness" was intimately connected with his evaluation of people.

Notes

1 *Goethe's Conversations*, People's Literature Publishing House, 1978, P. 112
2 *Commentary on the Thirteen Classics*, World Bookstore photocopy of the Ruan woodblock print, P. 2461
3 *Commentary on the Thirteen Classics*, World Bookstore photocopy of the Ruan woodblock print, P. 2469
4 *Laozi* Chapter 8 *Collected Works of the Philosophers*, Vol. 3, Shanghai Bookstore, 1991, P. 4
5 *Laozi* Chapter 27 *Collected Works of the Philosophers*, Vol. 3, Shanghai Bookstore, 1991, P. 15
6 Hong Xingzu [Song Dynasty]: *Additional Commentary on the Songs of Chu*, Vol. 1, Zhonghua Book Company, 1983, P. 18
7 Hong Xingzu [Song Dynasty]: *Additional Commentary on the Songs of Chu*, Vol. 4, Zhonghua Book Company, 1983, P. 154
8 *Annals of Yan Ying*, Vol. 6: "Oranges which grow south of the Huai River are real oranges, but those which grow north of the Huai are bitter. Their leaves are different, and so are their tastes. What is the reason for this? It is because the water and soil are different." *Collected Writings of the Four Basic Branches of Literature* photocopy of a Ming Dynasty woodblock print
9 Hong Xingzu [Song Dynasty]: *Additional Commentary on the Songs of Chu*, Vol. 1, Zhonghua Book Company, 1983, P. 47
10 "Offered to Li Yong", *Complete Works of Li Taibo*, Vol. 9, Zhonghua Book Company, 1977, P. 511
11 "Offered to Zhang Xianggao", Second Part *Complete Works of Li Taibo*, Vol. 11, Zhonghua Book Company, 1977, P. 599
12 "Ode to a Chivalrous Swordsman", *Complete Works of Li Taibo*, Vol. 3, Zhonghua Book Company, 1977, P. 216
13 *Ancient Style* 12, *Complete Works of Li Taibo*, Vol. 2, Zhonghua Book Company, 1977, P. 103
14 "An Imitation of the Lyrics With Which Bixie Trumpeters and Drummers and Zhiziban Singers Perform", *Complete Works of Li Taibo*, Vol. 3, Zhonghua Book Company, 1977, P. 238
15 "Reading a Book of the Art of War at Night", *Lu You's Collected Works * The Jian Nan Poetic Manuscripts*, Vol. 1, Zhonghua Book Company, 1976, P. 5
16 "Written on the Rainy and Windy Fourth Day of the 11th Month", *Lu You's Collected Works * The Jian Nan Poetic Manuscripts*, Vol. 26, Zhonghua Book Company, 1976, P. 710
17 "Written While Drinking on the Tower", *Lu You's Collected Works * The Jian Nan Poetic Manuscripts*, Vol. 8, Zhonghua Book Company, 1976, P. 213

3   The spirit of optimism

The spirit of optimism in Chinese literature is rooted in the philosophical outlook of ancient China. In the *Book of Changes* it says, "When the limit of emptiness is reached, then comes change. On the basis of change comes penetration."[1] In the *Laozi* it says, "Calamity, that's what fortune rests on. Fortune, that's what calamity rests on."[2] From the viewpoint of the Chinese, the depth of adversity is the beginning of good fortune, and the dawn always follows the darkest part of the night. It is under the influence of this point of view that Chinese literature often views and describes human life.

This can be most clearly illustrated in the field of the drama. It cannot be denied that in China there is very seldom seen the fearful and lamentable tragedy produced by the ancient Greek theater, which makes fate all-powerful. Chinese drama often has a happy ending, called a "grand reunion." For instance, an injustice is finally rectified, or a person cruelly murdered comes back as a ghost to take revenge, or a talented young scholar and beautiful maiden are separated, only to be united in marriage in the end. Whenever the hero sinks to the depths, we know that he will end up soaring to the heights. Some stories that originally ended in tragedy in the course of being handed down gradually came to have happy endings. An example is Yuan Zhen's novel *The Story of Yingying*, in which Yingying, the heroine, is abandoned by her lover, but in the hands of Wang Shifu the story is given a happy reunion-type ending in his poetic drama work *The Western Chamber*. Later, this work came to bear the title, "Master Zhang's Happy Reunion." In the collection of novels titled, *Immortal Words for Awaking the World*, there is a story titled, *Miss Bai Crushed under Thunder Peak Pagoda*. The original story goes that Miss Bai, who is a supernatural snake, is held down beneath Thunder Peak Pagoda by the rascally monk Fa Hai so that she can never attain mortal form. However, in the later dramatization of the story, her son achieves the highest place in the national civil service exam, and frees his mother.

In the closing years of the Yuan Dynasty and the early years of the Ming Dynasty there appeared the classical "happy ending with a reunion" drama called *The Pavilion for Admiring the Moon*, by Shi Hui. The story tells of two families torn apart and later reunited by the vicissitudes of war. The protagonists of one family are the elder brother Jiang Shilong and his younger sister Jiang Ruilian, and those of the other family are Wang Zhen, imperial secretary of the Ministry of War, his wife and their daughter Ruilan. At that time many people were fleeing south to escape the Mongol invaders, including the two Jiangs and Wang Ruilan and her mother, who travel together. In the crush of panic-stricken refugees, the two families become separated. When Jiang Shilong cries out in distress, "Ruilan! Ruilan!" The girl thinks that her mother is calling her. When she discovers that it is the young scholar the two travel together, pretending to be man and wife. Meanwhile, Jiang Ruilian accidentally meets Wang Ruilan's mother, and they too travel together. In the course of many adventures on the way, Jiang Shilong and Wang Ruilan fall in love, and, with the assistance of an innkeeper, get married. Jiang Shilong then falls ill. Wang Zhen, who is returning from a scouting expedition, happens to stop at the inn, and there sees his daughter. Disapproving of her marriage to Jiang Shilong, he forces her to accompany him, leaving her husband at the inn. Later, Wang Zhen meets his wife and Jiang Ruilian, so the Wang family is united once more. At this time the Mongol army is in retreat, but this happy state of affairs is marred for Jiang Ruilian, who is anxious about her brother, and Wang Ruilan, who worries about what has become of her husband. One evening the two girls pour out their grief under the moon. Before long, thanks to the care extended by a friend, Jiang Shilong recovers from his illness, and, in the company of that friend, journeys to the capital to take the imperial examination, from which they pair emerge top of the list in the civil and military examinations, respectively. Wang Zhen receives an imperial commission, and accepts the two youths as his sons-in-law. And so, after a number of adventures brother and sister and husband and wife are reunited, and *The Pavilion for Admiring the Moon* concludes with two weddings.

Stories like that of *The Pavilion for Admiring the Moon* we can call "great reunion" stories. This type of story is very common in Chinese drama, and there are many works in this genre, such as the famous drama *The Peony Pavilion* by Tang Xianzu of the Ming Dynasty. The plot is reminiscent of Shakespeare's *Romeo and Juliet*, except that the ending is different. In *The Peony Pavilion* the heroine, Miss Du Li, dies and comes back to life, and the love between her and Liu Mengmei is restored in a satisfactory conclusion. In *Romeo and Juliet*, the heroine, Juliet, also dies and comes back to life, but she finds that her lover Romeo has committed suicide. She then follows him in death.

The works of the great Chinese dramatist Guan Hanqing are also suffused with the spirit of optimism. Vulnerable people who are insulted and bullied finally triumph over their oppressors. Guan Hanqing thus gives hope and encouragement to his audiences, reluctant to leave them with a deep sense of alienation. In some of his plays there is a deep disparity in the strengths of those in the right and those in the wrong, and the spectators are sure that the play will end in tragedy. But, beyond everybody's expectation, Guan Hanqing ensures that good triumphs over evil in the end. The conclusion of the play is a happy one. In *Saving the Dusty Wind*, singing girl Song Yinzhang falls into the clutches of the villain Zhou She, but is rescued by her sworn sister, another singing girl called Zhao Pan'er. The latter relies on her wits, courage and beauty to ensnare and overcome her adversaries, and save Song Yinzhang, ensuring an all-around satisfactory dramatic outcome. In *Pavilion Overlooking the River*, Yang, an imperial official, schemes to have Bai Shizhong executed and then steal his wife, Tan Ji'er. Forewarned, Tan Ji'er disguises herself as a fishwife, and while pretending to gut fish in the Pavilion Overlooking the River steals Yang's imperial identification tablet and foils his plot. In *The Injustice Done to Dou E*, the heroine Dou E is executed, but returns as a ghost and gains her revenge.

The "grand reunion" happy ending is not rare in old Chinese novels either. For instance, in *The Story of Li Wa* by the Tang Dynasty novelist Bai Xingjian, in the Ming Dynasty prompt book *Yu Tangchun in Distress Finds a Husband* and *Wanggui Convent* from *Strange Tales from a Chinese Studio* by Pu Songling of the Qing Dynasty, among many others, we find the "grand reunion." And this is what has led to the spread of these stories among the common people and their popularity.

However, as the drama and the novel started to become stereotyped, the "grand reunion" started to become a cliché, losing its impact and artistic appeal, and giving the readers merely some cheap comfort.

The spirit of optimism is prominent in ancient Chinese poetry and ballads too, in particular in a positive attitude to people and a warm love of life. China has both a tradition of worldly poets and hermit poets (the latter living in seclusion in mountains and forests), but there are few Chinese poems or ballads which actually spurn human life. Even the hermit poets did not reject life itself; they rather rejected the coarseness of society and official careers, seeking in nature to create an ideal life. Tao Yuanming was known as the "original recluse poet of all time."[3] Nevertheless, his rustic verses display no world-weariness, but affection for nature, for farming and for hard work. His poems are saturated with the breath of life, and farmhouses, chickens and dogs, bean sprouts and mulberry and hemp plants are the stuff of everyday existence to him. Under Tao Yuanming's writing brush everything is full of life and vitality. Wang Wei, a leading landscape poet of the Tang Dynasty, was influenced by Buddhism. In some of his poems can be detected a note of melancholy, but even in these there is a tingle of life. Let's take a look at what he says in his poem "My Retreat at Mount Zhongnan":

> My heart in middle age found the Way,
> And I came to dwell at the foot of this mountain.
> When the spirit moves, I wander alone,
> Amid beauty that is all for me.
> I will walk till the water checks my path,
> Then sit and watch the rising clouds.
> And some day meet an old wood-cutter,
> And talk and laugh and never return.[4]

Even though he lives in seclusion he can still take great delight in the natural scenery, where he finds life's inspiration and inexhaustible joy. Again, let's take a look at the sixth poem of his "Tianyuanle (A Happy Pastoral Life)" series:

> Raindrops of last night still linger on peach flower petals,
> And lush willows are now enshrouded in the morning fog.

> Before the servant gets up to sweep away the fallen blooms,
> And this hermit gets out of bed, orioles have begun singing.[5]

Here there is no trace of world-weariness.

Because he tends to reflect the sufferings of the common people, Du Fu often describes his own worries, and this perhaps causes some people to regard him as a pessimist. But in fact this is not true; a sturdy optimism is a leading trait of his ideological character. No matter how bad the situation or how unfortunate his personal circumstances, Du Fu never loses his confidence and never abandons his ideals; whether revealing the dark side of government or describing the woes of the common people, he still harbors hope in his breast. His representative work "The North Expedition" is a poem saturated with an optimistic spirit. At the time that he wrote it the two capitals (Chang'an and Luoyang) of the Tang Dynasty had fallen to the rebels led by An Lushan (756). Du Fu fled, and on the way from Fengxiang to Linzhou "all he met were the wounded, groaning and bleeding." His own family suffered from hunger and cold. But even so Du Fu did not despair; on the contrary, he "Looks up and sees the changing color of the sky/Feels at rest that the evil air is being dispelled." Confident that the empire would soon revive, he shouted, "How can the northern barbarians forever last?/For our imperial order and law are not to end." This was his most robust, most optimistic cry during those troubled times. In his poem "Ascending the Tower," he says,

> Spring comes from the Brocade River and covers the Universe,
> The world still changes like a white cloud over Mount Jade.
> May the imperial court remain fixed as the Pole Star,
> Bandits from the stay your invading hands![6]

Struggling against difficulties of all kinds, and at a time when his country seemed to be shrinking by the day, Du Fu described the latter as being loftier than the Pole Star in the heavens, and something which could never be extinguished. So we can see that Du Fu was never crushed by his deep afflictions. The two themes of melancholy and optimism are interlaced with each other in Du Fu's poems to form his unique style.

Notes

1 *Commentary on the Thirteen Classics*, World Bookstore photocopy of the Ruan woodblock print, P. 86
2 *Laozi* Chapter 58 *Collected Works of the Philosophers*, Vol. 3, Shanghai Bookstore, 1991, P. 35
3 Zhong Rong [Nan Chao Liang]: *Poetical Works*, Vol. 2 (of three), Ancient Literature Publishing House, 1954, P. 41
4 Zhao Diancheng [Qing Dynasty]: *Collected Works of Wang Youcheng With Notes and Comments*, Vol. 3, Shanghai Ancient Books Publishing House, 1984, P. 35
5 Zhao Diancheng [Qing Dynasty]: *Collected Works of Wang Youcheng With Notes and Comments*, Vol. 14, Shanghai Ancient Books Publishing House, 1984, P. 359
6 Chou Zhaozhi [Qing Dynasty]: *Du Fu's Poems With Detailed Commentary*, Vol. 13, Zhonghua Book Company, 1979, P. 1130

4   The esthetics of conciseness

The characteristics of a country's literature have a close connection with that country's culture. As Chinese culture is noted for its conciseness, so is its literature noted for its esthetics of conciseness.

The question of conciseness is brought up in *Carving a Dragon with a Literary Heart*, China's first systematic work of literary criticism. In its "Hidden Elegance" chapter, it says, "Hiddenness is the body. Meaning comes from outside the words. The secret and the echo emerge side by side. The submerged brilliance glimmers in the depths. Like the divination trigrams which constantly change their shapes, like pearls and jade in the bed of a stream."[1] What this basically means is that the meaning exists separately from the words themselves, like a secret sound which comes from beside the words, a recondite coloring which hides its brilliance and changes from one shape to another, just like the trigrams of the *Book of Changes*, which change into each other. Here, "hiddenness" does not mean obscurity but conciseness. The intention is not to withhold knowledge but to avoid stating it too openly. It is a precise combination of the expressiveness and suggestiveness of language aimed at conjuring up the mental connection of the reader so that he discovers and grasps the quintessential profundity of the meaning. This is the artistic quintessence of Chinese literature. Sikong Tu was a leading poetry theorist of the late Tang Dynasty. In his "Discussions of Poetry with Li Sheng" he raises the topics of "the taste outside the flavor" and "the goal beyond the rhyme." In his "Conversations with Ji Pu" he raises the topics of "the symbol outside the symbol" and "the scene outside the scene." In his *Twenty-four Poems* he talks about "plumbing the depths of romance without using a single word." What he meant by this was that a poet must seek to awaken in the reader boundless imagination which transcends the bounds of mere words. The famous Song Dynasty poet Mei Yaochen said, "One must be able to describe scenes difficult to depict as if they were right before one's eyes, and concepts that cannot be contained in words. Only then can one reach the goal."[2] The Qing Dynasty literary theorist Ye Xie said, "The destination of a poem is elegance in a boundlessly succinct form. The thought should hover vaguely on the horizon, its purport lying between what can be expressed and what cannot. It points to the meeting of what can be explained and what cannot. The words are in one place and the meaning is in another. The thread of the meaning vanishes as it departs from shape. It becomes something beyond discussion and even thought. When it transports a person to a misty realm then it has reached its goal."[3] By stressing the meaning outside the words, the theorists point out that words are limited but meaning is not. This is a characteristic that Chinese literature shares with Chinese art as a whole. When the ancients talked about the "Spring and Autumn Style" of writing they were referring mainly to conciseness of language.

Ancient Chinese lyric poetry, because it is very short, puts great stress on conciseness, and demands a long view from a short passage, the perception of something big in something small and extended meaning from familiar words, i.e., limitless conciseness. For instance, "Fishing in Snow" by Liu Zongyuan of the Tang Dynasty:

> From hill to hill no bird in flight,
> From path to path no man in sight.
> A straw-cloaked man afloat, behold!
> Is fishing alone on river cold.[4]

The first two lines make no mention of the snow, just that there are birds flying in the hills and that there is no trace of human beings. Thus, the reader can imagine a scene of a world covered in snow. Against this background, the poet places a solitary boat and a fisherman clad in a straw cape and hat. Fishing rod in hand, he angles as usual in the snow-bound river. Carefree and at peace, he is unaffected by the changes in the outside world. This kind of independent, sticking to one's own way type of sentiment, which is implicit in the individual words and lines, is very thought-provoking.

Again, Li Bai's famous poem "On Hearing Jun the Monk from Shu Play His Lute":

> The monk from Shu with his green silk lute-case,
> Walking west down Emei Mountain.
> Has brought me by one touch of the strings,
> The breath of pines in a thousand valleys.
> I hear him in the cleansing brook,
> I hear him in the frosty bells.
> And I feel no change though the mountain darken,
> And cloudy autumn heaps the sky.[5]

This poem, which has five characters to a line, is about listening to a monk from what is now Sichuan Province play his lute. Jun is his Buddhist name. The first two lines tell us that the musician is from the west, Mount Emei in Sichuan. Li Bai himself grew up in Sichuan, the charming scenery of which cultivated his broad-ranging aspiration and stimulated his artistic imagination. He wrote several poems in praise of Mount Emei. As he was so attached to his home region it is not surprising that he should feel a special affection for a musician from there. And so this poem starts by introducing the lute player as being from his home area – he is a "monk from Shu" (Shu is an ancient name for Sichuan and its environs). He is carrying "green silk." Now "green silk" was originally a name for a lute. In fact, the Han Dynasty scholar Sima Xiangru had a lute named "green silk." Here it is used as a general term to indicate a high-class lute. The mere 10 characters used in the first two lines adequately picture the elegance of the musician and the admiration for him on the part of the poet.

The next line starts with a direct description of the monk's playing the lute, using the two characters "hui shou." This combination comes from *Fu Verses for the Lute* by Ji Kang, who says, "When Boya plucked the strings Zhong Qi heard the sound." The line "Has brought me by one touch of the strings/The breath of pines in a thousand valleys" compares the reverberations of nature to the music of the lute and brings to the reader the sonorous vigor of the latter. Moreover, there is a tone of wonder added by the poet when he says that "one touch of the strings" alone brought him "The breath of pines in a thousand valleys."

When Li Bai says, "I hear him in the cleansing brook" these words have the surface meaning of the poet's heart being delighted and refreshed upon hearing the monk playing the lute. However, there is a deeper meaning, which derives from a story in the ancient classical history *Spring and Autumn Annals of Mr Lv*. In Volume 14 of this work it says, "Formerly there was a musician called Boya, whose lute playing was particularly fine. However, only his close friend Zhong Ziqi was able to fully appreciate his skill. When Boya played his lute, his aspiration soared as high as Mount Tai. Zhong Ziqi said, 'Magnificent is your lute playing – as lofty as Mount Tai!' After a while, Boya's aspiration changed to that of a rushing stream, and Zhong Ziqi exclaimed, "Just like the rippling waters!" The sound of the lute formed a channel of connection for the thoughts and feelings of the two men. When Zhong Ziqi died, Boya smashed his lute and broke the strings, and never again played the lute, having lost the only person who could appreciate his music. It is in this tale that the proverb "High mountains and rippling waters" originates. In the above poem Li Bai harks back to the story of Boya and Zhong Ziqi to imply that it is through the medium of music that he and the monk share each other's feelings. "I hear him in the cleansing brook" is a model of conciseness, and it is also very natural. Although it is based on a classical tale it is not at all obscure, and displays Li Bai's outstanding skill with language.

"I hear him in the frosty bells" also has a classical reference. In the *Classic of Mountains and Seas * Central Mountains Classic* it says, "There are nine bells on Mount Feng. They chime every time the frost descends." This is the origin of the phrase "frosty bells." That Li Bai hears the sound of the lute in autumn is clear from the last line: "And cloudy autumn heaps the sky." "Frosty bells" also hints at the season. "I hear him in the frosty bells" means that even when the tune finishes the echoes linger on and on, and melt into the sound of the temple bells at twilight. In the *Tang Wen* chapter of the *Liezi* we find, "The echoes lingered around the rafters for three days." In his "Verses on the Red Cliff," the Song Dynasty poet Su Dongpo says, "The echoes curl away thinly, like delicate threads." He is referring to the sound of a bamboo flute, and conjures up an image of a listener to music in a deep reverie of artistic enjoyment even after the tune stops. "I hear him in the frosty bells" presents the same image; the crisp and smooth sound of the lute little by little becomes faint and distant, and together with the tinkling in unison of the evening bells, one becomes aware of the onset of evening. Writing "And I feel no change though the mountain darken/And cloudy autumn heaps the sky," the poet looks around after the monk from Shu stops playing his lute, and perceives that dusk from he knows not when has descended on the green mountain, and the grey clouds of autumn have piled up in the sky. Time passes so quickly! We all experience this – while we are absorbed in a drama or piece of music time seems to pass especially quickly. One hour, two hours are gone in a flash. If a performance is held in the afternoon you may enter the theater in blazing sunshine, but when you come out, with your feelings completely overwhelmed by what you have been watching, it is already time to light the evening lamps. This is exactly what "And I feel no change though the mountain darken/And cloudy autumn heaps the sky" expresses. It is perfectly apt and not exaggerated. The language used in this poem is pithy to a degree, but the sentiment it expresses is very profound and rich. It is full of meaning and very thought-provoking. In fact, this poem is a good example of "conciseness."

Both novels and dramas in China have this fine quality of conciseness. *The Scholars* by Wu Jingzi is a famous satirical novel, the satirical method of which relies on indirectness and conciseness. The author does not express his praise and blame, approval and disapproval directly; these are lodged in the concrete description. The leading modern writer and critic Lu Xun said of *The Scholars*: "It is indirect but biting." By "indirect" he was pointing out the novel's quality of conciseness. He says of a scene in which Fan Jin, who is supposed to be observing a three-year mourning period for his deceased father, eats a large shrimp dumpling: "There is not a word of censure, but the author's real sense of disapproval comes out quite clearly. In his subtle choice of words, the author takes deadly aim at his objective."[6] This comment points out in a concrete way the characteristic of conciseness in *The Scholars*. China's most famous novel, *A Dream of Red Mansions*, is also distinguished for its conciseness. The authors, traditionally Cao Xueqin and/or Gao E, invoke deep reflection in the reader through a series of concise descriptions of daily life that criticize the rottenness of the feudal ruling class. When we read this novel we often feel that the author has applied the techniques and symbolism of the Chinese poetry and ballad tradition to the creation of this novel. It has the indirectness and conciseness of poetry; it comes very close to Chinese poetry and is the supreme representative of the special feature of Chinese literature.

Notes

1 Fan Wenlan: *Carving a Dragon With a Literary Heart Annotated*, People's Literature Publishing House, 1978, P. 633
2 See *Ouyang Xiu's Notes on Poems, Notes on Poems Through the Ages* original text, Zhonghua Book Company, 1981, P. 267

3 Huo Songlin (chief editor): *The Latter Half of the Main Part of the Origin of Poetry*, People's Literature Publishing House, 1979, P. 30
4 *Collected Works of Liu Zongyuan*, Vol. 43, Zhonghua Book Company, 1979, P. 1121
5 *Collected Poems of Li Taibo*, Vol. 23, Zhonghua Book Company, 1977, P. 1129
6 Lu Xun: *A Brief History of the Chinese Novel, The Collected Works of Lu Xun*, Vol. 9, People's Literature Publishing House, 1973, P. 370

Part II

The division of Chinese literature into time periods

5   The basis for division into time periods

What is the basis for the division of Chinese literature into time periods? For many years it has been popular to make the time-period divisions of Chinese literature correspond to China's historical periods of social development – such as slave society literature, feudal society literature, semi-feudal/semi-colonial society literature, etc. Such period divisions are suitable for a sociological study of literature and for explaining the connection between literature and its socio-economic base. These are definite advantages, but this method is not the only one. For one thing, the use of this classification does not throw any light on the laws of development of literature itself. And this is not even to take into account the fact that the very division of ancient Chinese society into time periods is still a vexed question. The different views on such time periods of necessity make it difficult to produce a solid basis for time periods as applied to literature. Therefore, this book seeks a different standard for such time divisions, paying particular attention to the evolution of literature, which naturally demands the prominence of the evolutions of genres of literature.

In ancient China the evolution of literary genres was not simply a matter of the evolution of the forms of language; it was closely connected with the changes in the socio-economic base, in social practices and in cultural psychology. It also had some connection with political life. For instance, the flourishing of the writings of the various thinkers had a direct connection with the "hundred schools of thought contending" of the Warring States Period, and the *fu* style of poetry arose, flourished and had an important link with the reunification of China under the Han Dynasty. The heyday of the vernacular novels and dramas had a close connection with the prosperity of the urban economy in China and the demand for entertainment of the town-dwellers. Taking the evolution of genres as the basis for the demarcation of the time divisions of literature would seem to neatly reflect at least one aspect of social changes, and be a better way of indicating time periods than rigidly sticking to the history of social development.

The evolution of literary genres is an important aspect of the development of literature itself. The flowering of the literature of a certain period is often connected with the maturity of a certain genre, and the latter is often a symbol of that flowering. Examples are the poetry of the Tang Dynasty, the *ci* poems of the Song Dynasty and the drama of the Yuan Dynasty. Moreover, the coming to maturity of a certain literary genre is often accompanied by a new literary age; the influence of the coming to maturity of the novel on the literature of the mid-Tang period goes without saying, as does the coming to maturity of the poetic drama on the literature of the Yuan Dynasty. In each literary period a certain genre occupies a leading position, and to a great extent defines that period. Whether the literary form is elegant or down-to-earth, ostentatious or succinct this is always connected with the prominent genre of the time. Each literary genre has a relatively stable structure. It also has a consistent series of contents and method of expression. So, although the various writers who use a particular genre may have their own styles, viewed as a whole, the specific differences between the genres are marked. Thus the extravagant language of the Han Dynasty *fu* poems could not be transferred to the short lyric form of poetry, and the earthy language of the early vernacular novels could certainly not be used for parallel prose works. As for poems in the classical style, no matter how much they used common language they could never bring out the flavor of the *sanqu* songs. Likewise, the style of poetry that uses seven characters to the line may strive to be archaic and abstruse, but it can in general not equal the degree of those qualities attained by poems which use four characters to the line. Literature is an art using language, and genre is a condensation of a form of language. With the development of literary studies, we have to conclude that a firm grasp of genre as a link in the evolution of literature is very important.

In the course of the evolution of genres in Chinese literature, the following characteristics appear:

First, every genre of Chinese literature has its gestation, maturation and declination periods, just like a living organism. Generally speaking, its maturation period is short, like the blossoming of a flower. In a comparatively short period of time, a number of excellent works are produced, fully displaying the latent powers of expression of the genre. However, later generations are able to do no more than imitate these works, and the genre begins to decline. Writers tend to want to switch to another genre that is then in its gestation period. They abandon experimentation and exploration and seek to produce mature works in imitation of the maturation period of this new genre. The outstanding writers of ancient China tended to appear at about the same time, while at other times they are comparatively rare – like the ebb and flow of a tide. Just as sometimes the sky is full of twinkling stars, so does literature flourish, and when only a few lonely stars appear, so is the literary stage forlorn. During the Kaiyuan and Tianbao reign periods (713–756) of the Tang Dynasty, a number of master poets sprang up, but, following the death of Du Fu, the poetic stage once bestrode by such celebrated poets as Han Yu and Bo Juyi became a bare and shabby place. As for the short story genre, which emerged in the mid-Tang period, there is little of note, with the exception of masterpieces such as *The Story of Li Wa* and *The Story of Huo Xiaoyu*. In the late Tang short story creation was definitely losing its luster, and in the succeeding Song Dynasty seemed to be on its last legs. The peak of this genre had passed, and it is not difficult to understand why. Partly, it was due to social reasons, but the law of evolution of literary genres also had a part to play: If a person lived in a period of florescence of a certain literary genre, then his chances of becoming a great writer in that genre were comparatively great. But if he lived in a time when a genre was decaying and a new genre had yet to come to fruition, he would find it difficult to make a name.

Second, the various literary genres, in the course of their development, often blended and mingled with each other. After a particular genre reached maturity and sought to develop further, it often attracted characteristics from other genres. Just as in the science of botany hybridization is used to produce new species, the introduction of the stylistic characteristics of other genres was commonly used to inject new vigor into genres that were heading for decay. The *fu* poetry of the Han Dynasty, over a period of over 300 years until the end of that dynasty gradually became ossified, but received a new lease on life by incorporating the lyric features of the newly emerging "small *fu*." The *fu* genre was stimulated once more by the florescence of the parallel prose genre of the Southern Dynasties Period. By adopting the techniques of balance and tonal patterns from the latter, the genre of "parallel *fu*" developed.

Thirdly, the new literary genres were often conceived and born among the common people. Four-line, five-line and seven-line verse, as well as *ci* and *qu* lyric verse and vernacular novels all came into existence this way, and it is possible that the *sao* style of verse of the poet Qu Yuan had the same origin. When a new style of literature starts to circulate among the people it is not long before it attracts the attention, study and experimentation of the literati. It then goes on to become a new genre fashionable among the literati themselves. As writers expanded their fields of study and technical advances were made, a genre would reach its zenith of vigor. But as this progress continued, the structure of this genre could become rigid, with increasingly more attention paid to its rules and forms until it became ossified and stagnant. It would embark on a process of decline. At this time writers bold in experimentation would turn their eyes to some other form of folk literature and initiate a new form of study, experimentation and creation. This was how *shi* poetry changed into *ci* poetry and *qu* lyrical verse grew out of *ci* poetry.

6   The periods of Chinese literature

Based on an understanding of the above, we can tentatively divide classical Chinese literature into three periods: pre-Qin, Qin and Han Dynasties (until the third century AD); Wei and Jin Dynasties until the mid-Ming Dynasty (third century to 16th century; and mid-Ming to the "May 4th Movement" (16th century to early 20th century). And these three periods of classical Chinese literature can also be called the ancient period, medieval period and early modern period. The New Literature Movement of May 4, 1919 marks the start of the modern literature period, which has lasted to the present time.

The ancient period encompasses the pre-Qin and the Qin-Han eras. This was the time of gestation for all kinds of literary genres. The four-character verses of the *Book of Odes*, the *sao*-style verses of the *Songs of Chu* and the five-character verses of the Han Dynasty's Music Bureau are the three wellsprings of China's poetry and ballads, which laid the groundwork for the mainly lyrical tradition of this genre, just as prose writings such as the *Zuo Zhuan*, *Zhuangzi* and *Records of the Historian* laid it for classical Chinese prose. The concise and pithy nature of the latter had a great effect on the literary and artistic tastes of later generations. The myths and legends of the pre-Qin era are the source of the Chinese novel, and occupy a position by no means negligible. Moreover, the philosophical thought of those days (including attitude to life and value system), especially Confucianism and Taoism, which influenced Chinese literature took shape in this era. Concepts such as "verse expresses one's true intentions," "pure thoughts," "gentle and honest" and "Dao works the way nature does," which spring from Confucianism and Taoism, had a long-term and direct influence on the development of Chinese literature.

The ancient period can be divided into two stages:

In the first stage, that of the pre-Qin, there was no complete separation between literature, history and philosophy, or between poetry, music and dancing. This was the basic pattern of literature at that time. The *Book of Odes*, *Songs of Chu*, *Analects*, *Mencius*, *Laozi* (*Daodejing*) and *Zhuangzi* are all representative works of this stage.

In the second stage, that of the Qin and Han Dynasties, poems of five or seven characters to a line appeared, along with a large number of authors. This is the most notable phenomenon of this period. In addition, the *fu* poetry of the Han

Dynasty, with its extravagant style, well matched the atmosphere of the time, when that dynasty united the empire. The Han Dynasty's Music Bureau and Sima Qian's *Records of the Historian* represent the highest literary achievements of this stage.

The stage of classical Chinese literature which extended from the Wei and Jin Dynasties through the Sui, Tang, Song and Yuan Dynasties, to the middle period of the Ming Dynasty (1368–1644) was a period when all the important literary genres emerged and flourished. If we regard the Wei and Jin Dynasties as the starting point of the classical period, we must take into account the following factors: the beginning of a literary self-consciousness; the transformation of language from being archaic and abstruse to being more colloquial and easy to understand; the spread of literary creation to all strata of society; the spread of literary works by all sorts of well-developed means – hand-copying, printing, singing and performing.

The classical period can be divided into three stages:

The first stage of the middle period of Chinese classical literature lasted from the time of the Wei and Jin Dynasties until the middle of the Tang Dynasty (until the end of the Tianbao reign period of Emperor Xuanzong). This was the time when both the ancient- and modern-style verses of five and seven characters to a line emerged, took shape and reached their zenith. *Fu* poetry too made its greatest strides in this period – from the *da fu* poetry of the Han Dynasty, which developed through the Wei and Jin and Southern Dynasties periods to become the "parallel *fu*" of the Tang Dynasty. Along with the parallelism of the *fu* poetry went the same tendency in prose writings that produced parallel prose. From the "sturdy style of the Jian'an reign period (196–220 – of Emperor Xiandi of the Han Dynasty)" to the "heyday of the Tang Dynasty" two patterns of poetic and ballad creativity pervaded this whole period from beginning to end. From the Three Caos [Cao Cao, Cao Pi and Cao Zhi] to Du Fu, the thread of poetry and ballad creativity is clear and unbroken. Tao Yuanming, Li Bai and Du Fu are the three giants of this period. In fact, Du Fu rounds off this period and introduces the next. In addition, another phenomenon worthy of close attention during this period is the fact that individualism became more prominent as the mainstream trend of literary creativity and the influences of even metaphysics and Buddhism began to be felt in literature; thus the concept of literature became multi-faceted.

The second stage of the middle period of classical Chinese literature started in the mid-Tang Dynasty but fizzled out in the Southern Song Dynasty (1127–1279). In this stage the urban economy flourished, markets became enlivened and the urban population increased in number. With urban life at the center of things, new styles and interests emerged and gave rise to popular literature. Bo Juyi was a representative of the new development trend in literature which esteemed realism and common life. Poetry and ballads faced a particularly difficult situation following the death of Du Fu. It is true that Han Yu and Bo Juyi of the mid-Tang, Du Mu and Li Shangyin of the late Tang, and Su Shi and Jiang Xi of the Song Dynasty scored some heartening success in their efforts to blaze a new trail. But the new trend in Song poetry can be traced back to the mid-Tang, and poetry and ballads in this stage were marked by the identification of poets with scholars, an increase in literary discussion and poetry being permeated with themes of everyday life. The *ci* poetry, which had been popular and flourished during the mid-Tang, went through a process of refinement during the late Tang and Five Dynasties period, until it came into full bloom during the Song Dynasty, when it emerged as a literary genre in its own right, fit to be ranked alongside Tang poetry. As for prose writing, Han Yu and Liu Zongyuan of the Tang Dynasty championed a movement to write in the ancient style and promoted reforms in the fields of writing styles and language. Their achievements resonated for over 1,000 years – right up to the time of the May 4 Movement of 1919. The mid-Tang was also the time when the *chuanqi* novels [short stories mostly with fabulous plots] flourished, marking the maturity of the novel in China. New developments in this period were the "townsman's novels" of the Tang Dynasty and the storytelling folk art form of the Song Dynasty.

The third stage of the middle classical period stretched from the Yuan Dynasty (1206–1368) to the mid-Ming. There were two important developments in this stage: One was the rise to prominence of narrative literature, and the other was the fact that the target of literature was no longer confined to the scholar in his study, but expanded to include the audiences in the popular theaters. The latter, to a very great extent, guided the trend of literary creation at this time. The main representatives of literary achievements at this stage were the full-length novels *Romance of the Three Kingdoms* and *Outlaws of the Marsh*, and the dramas of such playwrights as Guan Hanqing, Wang Shifu and Gao Ming.

The late classical period started in the Jiajing reign period (1522–1567) of the Ming Dynasty. This was a watershed for literature. First of all, along with the development of the commercial economy, the burgeoning of the towns and increase in the urban population came the spread of printing and the increasing adoption by literary figures of the outlook of the townspeople. The result was that literary creation, at least partly, became a commercial activity. And in response to the new collective demands of the urban population, a series of changes took place in the subject matter, contents and tastes of literature. Secondly, under the influence of The Leftist School of Wang Shouren, writers began to flaunt their individuality and render a much more positive portrayal of human passions. Representative of literature in the Ming and Qing Dynasties are full-length novels with couplets introducing each chapter and grand dramas. The peak of literary achievement in this period is the novels *Journey to the West*, *Plum in a Golden Vase*, *The Scholars* and *A Dream of Red Mansions*, together with some short stories such as *The Peony Pavilion*, *Longevity Hall* and *The Peach Blossom Fan*. Thirdly, poetry, although not lacking in elegance in this period, produced no figures to compare with Li Dongpo and Du Fu. The Seven Pre-Ming and Seven Post-Ming Writers around the time of the Ming Dynasty praised the prose writings of the Qin and Han Dynasties and the poetry of the Tang Dynasty as the epitomes of their respective genres. But these people were only able to follow in the footsteps of their predecessors; they lacked creativity. Some Qing Dynasty poets studied the poetry of the Song Dynasty but were unable to produce anything fresh. At this point it became necessary for ancient literature to give way to modern literature and allow writers who had been baptized in the literary revolution known as the "May 4 Movement" to display their talents on the literary stage.

The recent classical period can be divided into two stages:

The first stage lasted from the beginning of the Jiajing reign period of the Ming Dynasty to the Opium Wars of the 1840s. This was the "bumper harvest" stage of the full-length colloquial novel, with *A Dream of Red Mansions* as the supreme achievement, and of the short story, with *The Peony Pavilion* as the pinnacle. As far as poetry is concerned, most importantly this stage witnessed contention between various schools.

The second stage of the recent classical period lasted from the Opium Wars to the "May 4th Movement." Following the Opium Wars China was plunged into the status of a semi-feudal, semi-colonized country. Western culture flooded in, and some Chinese intellectuals sought new literary experiences from the West, and from them sprang a group of writers with a global outlook. The main thread of literary endeavors was the quest to save the nation from doom and ensure its survival, and seek renewal from foreign lands. Literature came to be regarded as a tool for social betterment, and the social significance of the novel in particular was raised to a stage higher than it had ever enjoyed before. In the wake of the emergence of newspapers and the large-scale publication of translated works came a fundamental change in the means of literary expression.

Concerning the above discussion of the time periods of Chinese literature – seven stages of three general classical divisions – a more detailed examination can be found in the *History of Chinese Literature*, of which I was the general editor.[1]

Note

1 Yuan Xingpei (general editor): *History of Chinese Literature*, Higher Education Press, 1999, PP. 11–18

Part III

The regional nature of Chinese literature and the geographical distribution of literary figures

7   The regional nature of Chinese literature

As used here, the term "regional nature" has two meanings: One, individual literary genres sprang from different areas of China, and in the course of their development could not avoid the characteristics of these areas clinging to them. Two, the different areas of China had differences of literary style.

China covers a huge land area, and each region has its own natural conditions, manners and customs and sources of culture – all presenting definite differences. The regional nature of Chinese literature is apparent broadly in a north-south divide. The eastern and western parts of China also have their differences, to be sure, but they are not as pronounced as those between the north and the south. The large number of materials excavated in the course of cultural archeology attests to the fact that two cultures grew up respectively in the Central Plain of the Yellow River basin in the north and the Yangtze River basin (based on the states of Chu, Wu and Yue) in the south. Despite contacts between these two cultures, each preserved its special characteristics.[1] Besides these two, in the far south, in the areas of present-day Guangdong and Guanxi another distinct culture grew up. Confucian thought, including the contributions of Mencius, appeared in the north, in the states of Zou and Lu, whereas the Taoist thought of Laozi and Zhuangzi sprang up in the south, in the area of the Kingdom of Chu. The regional nature of pre-Qin philosophical thought has already been alluded to,[2] and a similar regionalism affected the literary output of this period. A phenomenon well worth noting in this regard is that Chinese literature displayed regional characteristics within the overall framework of the unity of the Chinese race.

The *Book of Odes* and the *Songs of Chu*, both products of the pre-Qin period, are works with very pronounced regional characteristics. The former is mainly a work of northern literature, while the latter had its roots in the south but still absorbed some northern literary nourishment. The simple and plain style of the *Book of Odes* and the romantic and passionate style of the *Songs of Chu* display the difference between the northern and southern approaches to literature, respectively. Discussing the differences in pre-Qin ideology and literature, Wang Guowei says:

> Theories of virtuous government in China prior to the Spring and Autumn Period can be divided into two schools of thought: monarchical and

non-monarchical. The former is represented chiefly by Confucius and Mozi, and the latter by Laozi. The former is a northern school of thought, and the latter a southern one. . . . In the following Warring States Period all philosophies stemmed directly from one or other of these two schools or were a mixture of the two. And so it is permissible to say that indigenous Chinese thought is restricted to these two schools. Chinese literature in this period likewise finds its expression restricted to these two trends of thought. The southern school produced only prose works, such as the works of the philosophers Laozi, Zhuangzi and Liezi. Poetry and ballads were mainly the province of the northern school of thought . . . The southern school did have some original poetic input – for instance, its imaginative power is far superior to that of the northern school . . . In fact, the production of great poetry and ballads required a combination of northern sentiment and southern imagination, and the poet Qu Yuan emerged as a product of this fusion.[3]

In the *Book of Odes* 15 of the poems or songs are classified as "Airs of the States." Some are identified with feudal states of that time, such as "Zheng Style" and "Qi Style"; some are identified with place names, such as "Bin Style." Bin was one of the earliest places of origin of the Zhou people. It was located in what is now Xun Township, Bin County, Shaanxi Province. The "King" in "King Style" refers to the Zhou capital after King Ping of Zhou moved to the east, i.e., ancient Luoyi, modern-day Luoyang and Meng Counties, Henan Province. Apart from the poems or songs titled, "Zhou Nan" and "Zhao Nan," which were produced in the south, in the region of the rivers Ru and Han, the other 13 "Airs of the States" are all northern folk songs. Confucius mentions the "lascivious music of the State of Zheng" (*Analects * Duke Ling of Wei*). When we take into account the fact that most of the "Zheng Style" airs were love songs, the regional coloring of their contents becomes clear. As for the "Paeans," such as the "Zhou Paean," "Lu Paean" and "Shang Paean," they were set to music to accompany the songs and dances when northern princes and aristocrats held ancestral sacrificial rites.

The very title of the "Songs of Chu" shows that it contains texts from the land of the Kingdom of Chu, and therefore the poems in it have a thick regional coloring. Huang Bosi of the Song Dynasty, in his *New Compilation of the Songs of Chu with a Preface*, says, "Everything in this book echoes the language, the sounds, the land and the things of Chu, and so it is also called the 'Words of Chu.'"[4] The *Songs of Chu* has an intimate connection with the geography, scenery, temperament, customs (such as rampant sorcery) and culture of the Kingdom of Chu. Particularly worthy of notice is the connection between the *Songs of Chu* and the fact that the folk songs of the Chu region were known as "Chu Songs" or "Chu Sounds." In the *Records of the Historian * Biography of Xiang Yu* by Sima Qian of the Han Dynasty we are informed that "One night Xiang Yu was surrounded by the Han army singing the songs of Chu."[5] In the *History of the Han Dynasty * Records of the Rites and Music* it says, "In the performance of music of any kind, the basic ritual requirements must not be neglected. Emperor Gaozu [Liu Bang, the founder of the Han Dynasty] was fond of the 'Chu Sounds,' and so his 'Chamber Music' was the 'Chu Sounds.'"[6]

And so we can see that the "Chu Songs" and the "Chu Sounds" were imbued with regional characteristics. In Liu Xiang's *Garden of Diction* *Fine Words*, there is a poem from the south called the "Song of the Yue Boatman":

> What a great night it is as I'm boating by the isles in the midstream.
> What a great day it is because I'm so honored to have the prince on board.
> I blush as I feel affectionate despite the guilt of infamy and possible insult.
> Oh prince, for a long, long time, I have felt this strong yearning to see you.
> While trees on the hills can feel their branches, my love you'll never know.[7]

The structure of this poem is different from that of the "Airs of the States." It has not a neat four-character arrangement. The lines are ended or sometimes broken by the "Xi" utterance, and it is here that we can see the root of the pattern used for the *Songs of Chu*.

The regionalism of Han Dynasty literature is likewise found in its poetry. *A Treatise Comprising a Mirror for Writing and a Repository of Rare Phrases * On Semantics* takes Sima Qian as the model for the northern style and Jia Yi as that for the southern style – as if there were two distinct schools of prose.[8] This is perhaps somewhat far-fetched. Nevertheless, Han Dynasty poetry and ballads do display a clear regionalism. The Music Bureau was an organization set up at the court to supervise music. It had been established previous to the reign of Emperor Wu (reign: 140–86 BC), but in his time it started to collect folk songs and musical performances on a large scale. In the *History of the Han Dynasty * Records of the Rites and Music* we find "When Emperor Wu set up the suburban sacrifices . . . He also established the Music Bureau. He collected folk poems and ballads (during the day) and went through them aloud in the evening, including songs from the States of Zhao, Dai, Qin and Chu."[9] Zhao, Dai and Qi were all in the north, while only Chu was in the south. But, according to the appendix to the *History of the Han Dynasty * Records of Art and Literature*, the Music Bureau did not confine itself to the above four states in its collection of poems and songs. There were also the *Fifteen Volumes of Songs and Poems from Wu and Chu, South of the Ru River, Four Volumes of Songs and Poems from South of the Huai River* and *Five Volumes of Songs and Poems from the Southern Prefectures*. There were also poems and songs from other parts of the south too. In his *Collected Poems of the Music Bureau*, Guo Maoqian of the Song Dynasty classifies Han Dynasty folk songs as "harmonizing songs," "songs to the accompaniment of percussion and wind instruments" and "songs to diverse tunes." The first was the common mode of the vulgar songs of the south, mainly Chu-area folk songs. The second was the musical mode of the peoples of the northern area in the time of Emperor Wu, mostly used as martial music at that time and with the words taken from northern folk songs. The third type may be compared to the "Deep in Thought" and "Shang Ye" songs from the *Eighteen Tunes for Songs Accompanied on the Cymbals* and the "Song of an Old Man" from the "Harmonizing Songs." The subject matter is the same but the style is different – the former stiff, the latter sentimental. And this is precisely the difference between the northern and southern styles.

During the period of the Southern and Northern Dynasties (386–589) the difference in the northern and southern literary styles was particularly marked. Wei Zheng says in his *History of the Sui Dynasty * Introduction to Anthology of Literary History:* "The cadence of the poets in South China is emotionally exciting, and therefore focuses on elegant forms. The rhyming scheme employed by the poets in North China is straightforward, and thus emphasizes substantive ethos. With substance, a poem is better reasoned than worded, and therefore of more practical use. With elegance, a poem is more rhetorical than expressive, and therefore fitter for chanting. Those are the major differences found in the poems written by poets of North and South China."[10]

The difference between the southern and northern literary styles is apparent in both poetry and prose. In the sphere of poetry and ballads the "Wu Songs," as the folk songs of the Southern Dynasties, were popular south of the Yangtze River. They center on the construction of the capital city at that time. They are love songs, dazzlingly tender and suitable for expressing the bashful and lingering emotions of a young girl. The "Western Melodies" were popular on the middle reaches of the Yangtze and in the cities on both sides of the Han River, centering on Jiangling. The themes are mainly the sorrowful thoughts of a traveller by water for his lady love. They chiefly display the life of boatmen and travelling merchants, and the keynote is a lingering sadness. The northern folk songs can be mostly found in the *Liang Drum and Trumpet Melodies.* These melodies refer to a vigorous type of martial musical performances done on horseback and featuring drums and trumpets. The northern folk songs originated in the various nationalities of the north. They represent the landscapes, customs and war-torn life of the north, yet there are also not a few love songs in a dashing and bold style, quite far removed from the folk songs of the Southern Dynasties.

To compare the way the two styles of the northern and southern folk songs, we can first cite an example from "Ziyege (Song of Midnight)," which belongs to the "Wu Songs": "The night is long, and sleeps eludes me. The moon is bright, and I seem to hear his voice. I answer only the empty air."[11]

Late at night, a sleepless lovesick girl fancies that she hears the voice of her lover calling to her. Without thinking, she calls out to him. She suddenly realizes that it was all a fantasy. This piece, from the collection of Northern Dynasties folk songs titled, "Popular and Willow Songs," aptly describes the scene: "Worry fills my heart. I have no joy. If I were my true love's whip I would be on his shoulder as he rides, by his knee when he sits."[12]

This is also a folk song about a girl thinking of her lover. She wishes she could be transformed into his horsewhip, so that she could always be by his side. The next folk song, only two lines, from "A Yuefu Song of the Diqu Style," is also about a girl thinking of her lover, but this time the note sounded is a straightforwardly happy one: "The moon is still bright but the stars are hanging low/Whether you'll come or not you'd better let me know."[13]

The clear difference between the elegance of the Southern Dynasties style and the bluntness of the Northern Dynasties style bespeaks a regional difference too. Although Liu Xie's *Carving a Dragon with a Literary Heart * The Physical*

World is a discussion of the wording used in literary creation, it still uses parallel prose and other literary flourishes:

> Spring and autumn roll around, succeeding one another, and the *yin* and *yang* principles alternately darken and brighten. When objects in the physical world change, our minds are also affected. When the *yang* principle begins to ascend, ants burrow, and when the *yin* principle congeals, the mantis begins to feed. Insignificant as these insects are, even they are affected. Profoundly indeed are things moved by the four seasons. Excellent jade inspires the mind of the intelligent, and glorious flowers shower splendor upon the soul that is pure. All things exert influence on one another. Who is there that can rest unmoved? Thus, as the new year is rung in and the spring begins to burgeon, we experience a joyous mood; as the luxuriant summer rolls by, our minds become filled with happy thoughts; as the sky heightens and the air becomes clear and brisk, our hearts become darkened and heavy with distant thoughts; and when the ground is covered with boundless sleet and snow, our souls are burdened with serious and profound reflections. Many different things appear in the course of the year, and each has a number of phases. One responds with varying emotions to these varying phases, and the form of language used depends on the emotion. One single leaf may suggest something significant, and the chirping of insects is often enough to induce an inner mood. So how much an influence will be felt if we experience a clear wind and a bright moon on the same night, or a bright sun and a spring forest on the same morning![14]

The writings of Yan Zhitui, who moved from the south to the north, are a blend of both southern and northern styles. There is no doubt that in his *Mr. Yan's Family Admonitions * Writings* his writing style has a northern coloring:

> Writing an article is like riding a fine horse. One may enjoy the feeling of being bold and unrestrained, but one must know how to rein in the horse with the bridle so as to prevent it from running astray from the tracks and falling into a ravine. An article can be comparable to a human body: Its argumentation resembles the heart and kidneys; its lofty presentation, muscles and bones; its content, skin; and its flowery language, a coronet. Contemporary followers of past writers are mostly superficially talented as they abandon their predecessors' fundamentals while embracing their incidentals. Rhetoric competes with and takes the upper hand of argumentation while quotation vies with creativity and suppresses the latter. Those who indulge themselves get too carried away, while those who want to patch up their far-fetched interpretations are not doing enough for a remedy. In a world of moral degradation like this, how can one be different? Only if things are not going too far.[15]

When China was once more united under the Tang Dynasty, which followed the short-lived Sui Dynasty, a golden age emerged in which there was a fusion of the southern and northern styles in both poetry and prose. Nevertheless, there was no shortage in the Tang Dynasty too of works with regional aspects. Examples are Cen Shen's "frontier poems," which have as their background the natural scenery of the northwest frontier. They reveal various aspects of army life, and in fact appeal to a broad spectrum of readers precisely because of this deep regional coloring. *Ci* poems, which in this period emerged as a new genre, also quite clearly had a regional tinge. The works of some *ci* writers of the mid-Tang who studied this poetical form produced by the common people often display a kind of southern mood. Zhang Zhihe of Jinhua, Wuzhou (modern Jinhua in Zhejiang Province) says in his "Yugezi (A Fisherman's Song)":

> In front of western hills white egrets fly up and down,
> Over [the] peach-mirrored stream,
> Where perches are full grown.
> In my broad-brimmed blue hat,
> And green straw cloak I'd fain,
> Go fishing oblivious of the slanting wind and rain.[16]

The background of this *ci* poem is Cihu Town, Wuxing County, Zhejiang Province, and its subject matter is the carefree life of a fisherman. This poem has a southern flavor to it, as do the nine poems in the "Bamboo Branch" collection, written by Liu Yuxi when he was dismissed from office and studied the folk *ci* of the southwest Ba and Chu regions, the three poems by Bai Juyi, who also studied folk *ci*, in his "Yijiangnan (Fair South Recalled)," the six in his "Langtaosha (Wave-Washed Sands)" and his "Everlasting Longing." We can take a glance at the last of these:

> See the Bian River flow,
> And the Si River flow,
> By Ancient Ferry, mingling waves, they go.
> The southern hills reflect my woe.
> My thoughts stretch endlessly,
> As does my heartache,
> So thus until my lover comes.
> Alone on moonlit balcony.[17]

Set in the misty scenery of the watery swamps of the lower Yangtze basin, this poem adequately expresses the longing of a lover far from home.

The focuses of the *ci* poems of both the late Tang and Five Dynasties Period (907–960) were on the south. The Huajian *ci* of the Sichuan region and the Feng and Li *ci* of southern Tang laid the foundation for the subtle style of this genre. At that time the north of China was in turmoil, while southern society was relatively stable and economically prosperous. At the same time, it cannot be denied that the geography, climate, scenery and manners of the south were conducive to the composition of *ci* poetry. For instance, "Spring water is as blue as the azure sky, Rain spattering on the slumbering barge."[18] "I dreamed of my South China home where plums were ripe. On awakening in a boat I played my flute in the rainy evening, While I overheard chitchatting on a bridge by a courier station."[19] "Girls wearing scent giggled upon one another's shoulders, vying for beauty and grace. Picking a lotus leaf each, they held it against the setting sun."[20] These poems are like landscape paintings, depicting the softness and charm of the southern region. The southern theme is preserved in Song Dynasty *ci* poems as well, but they are mature poems in themselves and display a variety of styles, so it is difficult to pin them down as to the characteristics of one particular area. Nevertheless, southerners abound among the Song Dynasty *ci* poets: Tang Guizhang, in his notes and commentary on the *Three Hundred Song Dynasty Ci Poems*, estimates that southerners make up about 64 percent of poets included in it. And so we can see from this how close the connection was between *ci* poetry and the southland.

As far as the drama which flourished during the Yuan Dynasty is concerned, both the style of its music and that of its language display regional differences. The poetic drama in four acts and with a prologue set to music (*zaju*) is an art form which arose in the north, and the creation and performance of this type of drama was centered on the capital Dadu (present-day Beijing). The most celebrated authors of *zaju* – Guan Hanqing and Wang Shifu – were both residents of Dadu. Two other famous playwrights of this time were also northerners – Zheng Guangzu was a native of Xiangling, Pingyang Town (near Linfen in present-day Shanxi Province), and Gong Tianting was a native of Daming (in present-day Hebei Province). As these instances indicate, *zaju* was a literary genre which had its roots in the three northern provinces of Shanxi, Hebei and Shandong, with Dadu as the center. Wang Guowei once said of the Yuan Dynasty *zaju* that "Of the 62 authors of zaju plays, 49 were northerners and only 13 were southerners. Of the northerners, 46 came from the provinces of Zhili (modern Hebei), Shandong and Shanxi, and of them 19 were residents of the capital. Moreover, nine out of ten of the 46 were authors of the first period of the *zaju*. . . . After the middle period of the Yuan Dynasty the authors of *zaju* drama were all residents of Hangzhou. Playwrights such as Gong Tianting, Zheng Guangzu, Zeng Rui, Qiao Ji, Qin Jianfu and Zhong Sicheng were, it is true, natives of the north, but they all lived for extended periods in Zhejiang Province (of which Hangzhou is the capital). So it could be said that the root soil of the *zaju* had shifted southward."[21]

When the *zaju* drama began to decline, in the south another form of drama began to flourish – the *nanxi*, or classical local opera. It emerged in the Wenzhou area of Zhejiang Province round about the close of the Northern Song Dynasty (960–1127) and the beginning of the Southern Song Dynasty. It first spread to Hangzhou, where it developed into a mature dramatic art form and flourished until the end of the Yuan Dynasty. The representative playwright of this genre was Gao Ming, a native of Rui'an (modern Wenzhou, Zhejiang Province). Concerning the difference between the northern and southern melodies, Wang Shizhen of the Ming Dynasty, in his *Flowery Tunes*, has this to say:

> Melodies in general: The northern ones tend to be wordy and hurried, and their staccato parts are muscular; the southern ones tend to have fewer words,

their pace is more languid, and they lend themselves to contemplation. The northern ones tend to be heavy on diction but light on expression, whereas the southern ones show the opposite tendency. The northern ones sound well when accompanied by stringed instruments; the southern ones by clappers. The northern ones are suitable for choral singing; the southern ones for solo singing. The northern ones verge on the uncouth; the southern ones on weakness.[22]

In his *Patterns of Melodies * Random Notes*, Wang Jide of the Ming Dynasty says something similar:

The southern and northern styles of melody are as different as chalk and cheese. The former is deep and bold, while the latter is soft and subtle. Each has its own restricted sphere: The northerners concentrate on creating whole works, while the southerners concentrate on crafting sentences. The former express themselves by means of vigor, while the latter express themselves by means of color and gloss.[23]

The above two passages discussing the difference between the southern and northern styles of melody are reminiscent of Wei Zheng's comment on the difference.

During the Ming and Qing Dynasties China was united, and the regionalism in literature was not as marked as it had been in the pre-Qin, Southern and Northern Dynasties or Yuan periods. But it can still be detected. The short story genre of the Ming Dynasty, which developed out of the regional operas of the Song and Yuan Dynasties are divided into the so-called "four big tunes," namely, the Haiyan tune, the Yuyao tune, the Geyang tune and the Kunshan tune. All of these are southern styles of singing or recitation. Most of the Ming Dynasty short stories have love as their theme. It was said that nine out of 10 dealt with "lovelorn longing," and this was a southern literary tradition.

There were even more regional schools of poetry in the Ming and Qing Dynasties, such as the "Chaling school" (named after Chaling County in modern-day Hunan Province), headed by Li Dongyang; the "Gong'an school" (named after Gong'an County in modern-day Hubei Province), represented by the brothers Yuan Zongdao, Yuan Hongdao and Yuan Zhongdao; and the "Jingling school" (named after a place in Tianmen County, Hubei Province), headed by Zhong Xing and Tan Yuanchun.

Kun opera, which originated in the Suzhou area, reached its maturity around the time of the demise of the Ming Dynasty and the early years of the Qing Dynasty, and eventually became the dominant drama form of the whole country. A group of playwrights gathered in Suzhou, of whom the representative was Li Yu, whose ideas as to artistic style were similar. They later came to be known as the "Suzhou school." Besides Li Yu, the "Suzhou school" boasted Zhu Zuochao and Ye Shizhang. In the Qing Dynasty, around the time of the Opium Wars (1840–1842) there arose the "Five Major Types of Tunes." These were, in addition to the already existing "Kun tune," the "High tune" (which had evolved from the

"Geyang tune" and included the styles of opera native to Hunan, Sichuan, Jiangxi and Guangdong), the "Clapper tune" (or "Qin tune," originating on the border between Shaanxi and Shanxi provinces and spreading to the northern area), the "Stringed-instrument tune" (originating in Henan and Shandong provinces) and the "Pihuang tune" (made up of the words *xipi* and *erhuang*, two types of traditional opera music, represented by the Hui style of Anhui Province and the Han style of Hubei Province). All these "tunes" exhibit clear regional characteristics, and their blossoming is a sign of the prosperity of drama in China.

The regionalism of Chinese literature enriched its style and appeal. However, while in some periods this regionalism was prominent, in others it tended to fade and become merged with the national characteristics of Chinese literature, in fact, adding a new component to these national characteristics.

Notes

1 *Library of Research into the Literature of the Yangzi River*, edited by Ji Xianlin, is a good reference work for a full description of this subject. It is divided into sections on literary archeology, academic thought, economy, science and education, literary art and social life. Hubei Education Press, 2004

2 See *Regionalism in the Development of Philosophy in Ancient China* by Ren Jiyu in *A Collection of Treatises on Chinese Scholarship*, Zhonghua Book Company, 1981

3 *The Spirit of Literature in Qu Zi*, in *Continued Collection of the Works of Jing An*, Vol. 5 of *Posthumous Works of Wang Guowei*, The Commercial Press, 1940, pp. 31–32

4 The original, in 10 volumes, has been lost. For the original preface see Vol. 92 of the *Mirror of Song Dynasty Literature*, Zhonghua Book Company, 1992, P. 1306

5 Sima Qian [Han Dynasty]: *Records of the Historian*, Vol. 7, *Biography of Xiang Yu*, Zhonghua Book Company, 1959, P. 333

6 Ban Gu [Han Dynasty]: *History of the Han Dynasty*, Vol. 22, *Records of the Rites and Music*, Zhonghua Book Company, 1962, P. 1043

7 *Fine Words*, Vol. 11 of *Garden of Diction*, Zhonghua Book Company, 1987, P. 278. The character for "boat" was originally that for "sandbar." The *Transcripts of the Northern Hall*, Vol. 106, recommends this change

8 In the "On Semantics" chapter of the South Section of *A Treatise Comprising a Mirror for Writing and a Repository of Rare Phrases* (original Japanese title being *Bunkyō Hifuron*), Kūkai comments, "While analyzing *Book of Changes*, Confucius put his thought into his *Appended Statements* annotations, which, though written in simple language, are of a vigorous poetic style. Confucius passed the style to his students Xia and You, who in turn passed it on to Xun Qing and Meng Ke. Xun and Meng then brought forth poems with four and five characters to a line, respectively, modeling them after the ancient classics. They later bequeathed the style to Sima Qian, who handed it down to Jia Yi. Banished to Changsha, Jia not only felt that he was a loser, but he also found himself unadaptable to the local customs. He then vented his anger on his superiors and resorted to rhetorical devices that lacked the flavor of "Airs of the States" and "Court Hymns." Following him were poets who all seethed with discontent and sarcasm. Sima Qian was then known to belong to the Northern School, while Jia Yi, to the South, thereby bringing forth two different traditions." (Kūkai, *Comprising a Mirror for Writing and a Repository of Rare Phrases*, proofread and annotated by Wang Liqi, China Social Sciences Publishing House, 1983, P. 278)

9 Ban Gu [Han Dynasty]: *History of the Han Dynasty*, Vol. 22, Zhonghua Book Company, 1962, P. 1045

10 Wei Zheng et al. [Tang Dynasty]: *History of the Sui Dynasty*, Vol. 76, Zhonghua Book Company, 1973, P. 1730

11 *Collected Poems of the Music Bureau*, edited by Guo Maoqian [Song Dynasty], Vol. 44, *Words for Qingshang Tunes*, Zhonghua Book Company, 1979, P. 643

12 *Collected Poems of the Music Bureau*, edited by Guo Maoqian [Song Dynasty], Vol. 25, *Words for Flute Tunes*, Zhonghua Book Company, 1979, P. 369

13 *Collected Poems of the Music Bureau*, edited by Guo Maoqian [Song Dynasty], Vol. 25, *Words for Flute Tunes*, Zhonghua Book Company, 1979, P. 367

14 Fan Wenlan: *Carving a Dragon With a Literary Heart Annotated*, Vol. 10, People's Literature Publishing House, 1978, P. 693

15 Wang Liqi: *Collected Explanations of Mr. Yan's Family Admonitions*, Vol. 4, Shanghai Ancient Books Publishing House, 1980, PP. 248–249. "Hasten to the End, Scorning the Essence" in the *Collected Works of Mr. Wang* was originally "Hasten to the Essence, Scorning the End". This has been corrected in the *Collected Works From Lack of Knowledge Studio*

16 *Complete Tang Poems*, Vol. 308, Zhonghua Book Company, 1960, P. 3491

17 Complete Tang Poems, Vol. 890 Zhonghua Book Company, 1960, P. 10057

18 Wei Zhuang [Tang Dynasty]: "Pusaman", Li Yimang's *Collected Teachings Among the Flowers*, Vol.3, People's Literature Publishing House, 1958

19 Huang Fusong [Five Dynasties]: "Mengjiangnan (Dreaming of the South)", *Collected Teachings Among the Flowers*, Vol. 2, People's Literature Publishing House, 1958

20 Li Xun [Five Dynasties]: "Nanxiangzi (Southern Village)", *Collected Teachings Among the Flowers*, Vol.10, People's Literature Publishing House, 1958

21 *A History of Song and Yuan Drama*, Vol. 9, "The Time and Place of Yuan Drama", *Posthumous Works of Wang Guowei*, Vol. 15, The Commercial Press, 1940, P. 60

22 *Collection of Theses on China's Ancient and Drama Music*, Vol. 4, China Theater Publishing House, 1959, P. 27

23 Wang Jide [Ming Dynasty]: *Patterns of Melodies*, Hunan People's Publishing House, 1983, P. 175

8 The geographical distribution of Chinese writers

This so-called "geographical distribution" comprises the following three scenarios:

1 In a certain period a particular region produced a crop of writers, making it a gathering ground for literary figures;
2 In a certain period writers concentrated their efforts on a particular region, making it a center for literature; and
3 In a certain period the number of writers produced by each region can be calculated.

Gathering together the above three situations, we can discover the following regions which have proved important in China's literary history:

Zou and Lu

Previous to the Qin Dynasty there are not many writers whose names and native places we know. Nevertheless, we can be fairly sure that the region comprising the states of Zou and Lu was a breeding ground of cultural activities. Among the pre-Qin prose works, we have the *Analects*, a book recording the words and deeds of Confucius, as well as of his disciples and others who carried on his teachings. Confucius' surname was Qiu, and his given name was Zhongni. He lived in the State of Lu in the Spring and Autumn Period. Mo Di, the author of the *Mozi*, was also a native of Lu. He was a philosopher and writer of a later generation than Confucius. The *Mencius* records the words and deeds of Meng Ke, a native of Zou (present-day Zou County, Shandong Province). About the *Zuo Zhuan*, a pre-Qin historical work by Zuo Qiuming, we find this comment in Sima Qian's *Records of the Historian * Chronologies of Twelve Rulers*: "The Lu gentleman Zuo Qiuming, fearing that those who came after Confucius would foster heretical views, each pursuing his own idea and losing sight of reality as it was, wrote *Mr. Zuo's Spring and Autumn Annals* as a gloss or explanation of the text of the history that Confucius wrote (the *Spring and Autumn Annals*)."[1] In the *History of the Han Dynasty * Records of Art and Literature* the following is recorded: "*Mr. Zuo's Annals* has 30 volumes. Zuo Qiuming, a leading historian of the State of Lu."[2] We can see from this that the Zuo-Lu area was fertile ground for literary activities in the pre-Qin period, and that this area was the wellspring of the plain northern literary style.

Jing and Chu

The *Laozi*, which contains only 5,000 words, can be regarded as a philosophical work written in verse. The basic line of thought of this book is the ideology of Lao Dan, who lived in the Spring and Autumn Period. Lao Dan himself was a native of Ku County in the Kingdom of Chu (modern Luyi, in Henan Province). The *Zhuangzi* is not only a philosophical work; it also has a high literary value. Its author, Zhuang Zhou, was a native of Meng, a district on the present border between Henan and Anhui provinces. He once served King Wei of Chu as prime minister. He carried on and developed Laozi's philosophy, and clearly belonged to the literary tradition of the region of Jing and Chu. China's first and greatest poet at the time, Qu Yuan, was also a native of the Kingdom of Chu. The outstanding characteristic of his poetry is his creation of individual poems out of a tradition of collective ones. His *sao* verse style, which he employed in his great collections of poems "Li Sao," "Nine Songs" and "Asking Heaven," had a profound influence on later generations. In the *Records of the Historian * Biography of Qu Yuan* we find, "Following the death of Qu Yuan, various schools of poetry drawing on inspiration from him, such as Song Yu, Tang Le and Jing Chai, became known for their poetry in the *fu* style."[3] In fact, as the Warring States Period drew to its close the Kingdom of Chu became the center of *fu* (or *cifu*) poetry.

Huainan

There was a close connection between the burgeoning of *fu* poetry during the Han Dynasty and its encouragement by the ruling group. "Wang Liu'an of the region south of the Huai River (roughly central Anhui Province to the Yangtze River) was an erudite man . . . who gathered around him thousands of scholars and other men of learning."[4] Among them were a number of *fu* poets. In the *History of the Han Dynasty * Treatise on Literature* we find, "Eighty two volumes of Wang-style *fu* poetry were produced in the Huainan region," and "Forty four volumes of *fu* poems were produced by poets of the Wang school in the Huainan region." We can infer from this how rich the writing of *fu* poetry was in the Huainan region at this time. Unfortunately, none of Wang Liu'an's *fu* poems have survived, and of those of his followers only the volume "Summoning the Hermit" by Xiaoshan of Huainan.

Chang'an

As the capital of the Han Dynasty, Chang'an naturally became a gathering place for the literati. Both Emperor Wu and Emperor Xuan (reign: 73–49 BC) encouraged the composition of *cifu* poetry, and a number of such poets were attached to their courts, including Sima Xiangru, Mei Gao and Dongfang Shuo. Other leading writers native to or based in Chang'an were Zhu Maichen, Yuqiu Shouwang, Yan Zhu, Zhufu Yan, Zhong Jun, Ni Kuan, Kong Zang, Dong Zhongshu and Sima Qian. Emperor Xuan's court was graced by Wang Bao, Zhang Ziqiao and Liu

Xiang, while the court of Emperor Cheng (reign: 32–8 BC) hosted Yang Xiong, the most celebrated *fu* poet of the later years of the Western Han Dynasty (206 BC–25 AD).

Yedu

Yedu was located in the northern part of Linzhang County, in Hebei Province. It was chosen by Cao Cao (a protagonist of the Three Kingdoms Period – 220–280) as his capital. It was a gathering place for a number of scholars in the Jian'an reign period at the end of the Han Dynasty. The leading figure among them was Cao Cao himself; others were Chen Lin, Wang Can, Xu Gan, Ruan Yu, Ying Chang, Liu Zhen, Cao Pi and Cao Zhi. While studying the Han Music Bureau collection, they wrote about social upheavals and the sufferings of the people and at the same time chanted about their own ideals and burdens. Thus was developed a forlorn and avid style, which later generations came to label the "vigorous Jian'an style." Zhang Shuo, a famous Tang Dynasty prime minister, wrote a poem titled, "Lured by Yedu," part of which runs: "[Cao Cao] by day led stalwarts to smash mighty armies, and by night presided over poetry salons."[5] Yedu was a unique center for the creation of poems and ballads in those days and attracted just about every poet in the country. The poems composed in the area and time of Shu and Wu (the southernmost of the Three Kingdoms) tended to be bleak and cheerless.

Jinling

Jinling (modern Nanjing in Jiangsu Province) was the capital of the Eastern Jin Dynasty and the Southern Dynasties, and became a center of literary activity, particularly during the latter's Liang and Chen Dynasties. The courts of Xiao Gang, Emperor Jianwen, of Liang and later Master Chen Shubao of Chen hosted groups of poets such as Xu Li of Liang and Jiang Zong and Kong Fan of Chen, and were veritable hives of literary creativity.

Henan

As the capital of the Tang Dynasty, Chang'an naturally attracted the literati of that period. However, most of these literary figures came from the region which is now Henan Province. This is worthy of special notice. The great poet Du Fu's ancestral home was in Xiangyang, but the family moved to Gong County in Henan, where Du Fu was born. Another leading poet of the dynasty was Han Yu, who came from Heyang, which is modern Meng County, also in Henan. It was said that "Du's poems and Han's writing brush" both originated in Henan. Apart from those two, Shen Quanqi came from Neihuang in Xiang Prefecture (modern Neihuang, Henan); Song Zhiwen from Hongnong in Guo Prefecture (modern Lingbao, Henan); Zhang Shuo, Wang Wan, Yuan Jie, Liu Fangping, Han Hong, Yuan Zhen and Nie Yizhong from Luoyang; Cui Hao from Bian Prefecture (modern Kaifeng, Henan); Li Qi, originally from Zhao prefecture, settled in Yingyang (near modern Xuchang, Henan); Cen Shen from Nanyang (modern Nanyang, Henan); Wang Jian from Yingchuan (modern Xuchang, Henan; Li He from Fuchang (modern Yiyang, Henan); Zhang Hu from Nanyang and Li Shangyin from Henei in Huai Prefecture (modern Qinyang, Henan). About half of the leading Tang poets came from Henan, and especially from Luoyang and Nanyang. Natives of Henan made a great contribution to the florescence of poetry during the Tang Dynasty. They were followed by poets from the Shanxi and Shaanxi areas, while comparatively few came from the Jiangnan region.

Jiangxi

During the Song Dynasty literary inspiration gravitated toward the south, and the Jiangxi region especially became a hotbed of literary styles. Yan Shu, Yan Jidao and Wang Anshi were natives of Linchuan (modern Linchuan in the Jiangxi Zhuang Autonomous Region); Ouyang Xiu and Liu Chenweng of Luling (modern Ji'an, Jiangxi); Li Gou of Nancheng (modern Nancheng, Jiangxi); Zeng Gong of Nanfeng (modern Nanfeng, Guangxi); Huang Tingjian of Fenning (modern Xiushui, Jiangxi); the "three Kongs" – Pingzhong, Wenzhong and Wuzhong – of Xinyu (modern Xinyu, Jiangxi); Yang Wanli and Wen Tianxiang of Jishui in Ji Prefecture (modern Jishui, Jiangxi); Liu Guo of Taihe, also in Ji Prefecture, (modern Taihe, Jiangxi); Jiang Kui of Poyang in Rao Prefecture (modern Poyang, Jiangxi) and Xie Fangde of Geyang in Xin Prefecture.

Dadu

Dadu, the Yuan Dynasty capital, was the heartland of the Yuan poetic drama (*zaju*), as most of the authors of those plays hailed from there. There is no need to repeat what has been related above.

Jiangzhe

In the Ming and Qing Dynasties literary creation flourished in the area of the Zhe River, roughly in the region of present-day Zhejiang Province, which produced writers in large numbers. Here it is only necessary to list their names, without going into details of their native places. The Ming writers from this region were Liu Ji, Gao Qi, Yu Qian, Wen Zhengming, Wang Pan, Chen Duo, Xu Wei, Wang Shizhen, Feng Menglong, Chen Zilong, Gu Yanwu, Zhang Huangyan, Xia Wanchun, Shi Nai'an and Wu Cheng'en. Apart from the so-called "Three Scholars of the Lower Reaches of the Yangtze River," namely, Qian Qianyi, Wu Weiye and Gong Dingzi, writers of the Qing dynasty also included Gu Yanwu, Wu Jiaji, You Dong, Chen Weisong, Zhu Yizun, Zha Shenxing, Shen Deqian, Li E, Zheng Xie, Yuan Mei, Zhao Yi, Huang Zhongze, Zhang Huiyan, Gong Zizhen, as well as Li Yu (with "Yu" meaning jade), Li Yu (with "Yu" meaning fishing), Hong Sheng and Yang Chaoguan. Most of them came from Suzhou, Yangzhou and Changzhou.

Lingnan

The focus of modern Chinese literature swung south to the Lingnan area (Guangxi and Guangdong). Zhang Weiping was a native of Fanyu in Guangdong Province (modern Fanyu, Guangdong); Huang Zunxian of Jiaying Prefecture (modern Mei County, Guangdong); Kang Youwei of Nanhai (modern Nanhai, Guangdong); Liang Qichao of Xinhui (modern Xinhui, Guangdong) and Su Manshu of Zhong-shan (modern Zhongshan, Guangdong).

Shu Zhong

This area has produced literary men since the Han Dynasty, and they have often been first-class writers. Sima Xiangru and Yang Xiong, of the city now known as Chengdu in Sichuan Province, were both natives of the Shu region during the Han Dynasty. The poet Li Bai of the Tang Dynasty moved to Mianzhou (in modern Jiangyou County, Sichuan) at the age of five, and called himself a man of Shu. The Song Dynasty father and sons Su Xun, and Su Shi and Su Zhe were natives of Meishan in Mei County (modern Meishan, Sichuan). While all these people were born or raised in the Shu Zhong area, they made their names outside it. Staying at home, they were nobodies, but as soon as they left their native region they soared to the highest position on the literary stage. So although the Shu Zhong area never became a center of literature, its role in nurturing literary figures should not be underestimated.

The above are interesting facts, to be sure, but what conclusion can we draw from them?

1. The areas where literature developed were generally comparatively eco-nomically well developed, society was relatively stable and there were rich col-lections of books. They were also areas where education was of a high standard. Some were political centers, while others were quite open transportation hubs. The Chang'an-Luoyang-Nanyang axis during the Tang Dynasty, the Gan River basin in Jiangxi Province during the Song Dynasty, the Zhe River area during the Ming and Qing Dynasties and Guangdong in modern times all met these criteria for centers of literary activity.

2. Chinese literature is an integral part of Chinese culture, but Chinese litera-ture and Chinese culture do not share one identical source. In fact, we ought to say that there were at least two sources for both – the Yellow River basin and the Yangtze River basin. Moreover, the center of Chinese literature moved by and large along lines which today connect from north to south Tianjin and Hangzhou, and Beijing and Guangzhou. From a broad historical perspective, we can view the various focuses of literary activity as being located along these two axes. From one perspective, this explains the importance of south-north communications on the development of Chinese literature. Throughout Chinese history the political center of the country has mostly been in the north, while the economic backup force has been in the south (especially from the Tang Dynasty onward). So long as the Grand Canal (which stretched from Hangzhou to Tianjin and the Beijing area)

remained open – and the feudal dynasties had no difficulty ensuring this – it was China's lifeline. And so it was natural that the centers of literary activity in China should grow up around the three great waterways of the Yellow and Yangtze rivers and the Grand Canal.

As well as historical accounts, textual criticism of writers' works and descriptions of literary styles, there is another important aspect of research into Chinese literature which is often overlooked, and that is regional studies. The present work is only a tentative first step; many questions await deeper treatment.

Notes

1 Sima Qian [Han Dynasty]: *Records of the Historian*, Vol. 14, Zhonghua Book Company, 1982, second printing, P. 509
2 Ban Gu [Han Dynasty]: *History of the Han Dynasty*, Vol. 30, Zhonghua Book Company, 1962, P. 1713
3 Sima Qian [Han Dynasty]: *Records of the Historian*, Vol. 24, Zhonghua Book Company, 1959, P. 2491
4 Ban Gu [Han Dynasty]: *History of the Han Dynasty*, Vol. 44, "Biography of the King of Huainan", Zhonghua Book Company, 1962, P. 2145
5 *Complete Tang Poems*, Vol. 86, Zhonghua Book Company, 1960, P. 939

Part IV

The categories of Chinese literature

In ancient China it was the constant practice to distinguish literary works according to subject matter and content. The *Selected Works of Literature* was the first to separate literature into genres – 39 of them. Later, subdivisions were added, for instance in the *fu* and *shi* poems, depending on subject matter and content. There were 15 subcategories of *fu* poems, including "capital," travelogue," "palace," "mourning" and "musical." Ouyang Xun of the Tang Dynasty, in his *Comprehensive Categories of Art and Literature*, classifies the whole of literature by subject matter and content, such as "Heaven," "time," "earth," "man," "trees," "birds," etc. Li Fang of the Song Dynasty, in his *Blooms in the Literary Garden*, follows the format of the *Selected Works of Literature* in his classification of literature according to subject matter and content. It is because there was this accepted practice in ancient China that an overview of Chinese literature must examine the question of categories from the angle of subject matter and content.

However, the categories covered by the *Selected Works of Literature* and *Comprehensive Categories of Art and Literature* are far from trivial and their standards are not identical. In fact, it cannot be said that there is a key thread that runs through them. Moreover, simplistic categories like Huang Zongyi's "Platform and Pavilion Writing" and "Mountain and Forest Writing,"[1] or Lu Xun's "Imperial Court Literature," "Mountain and Forest Literature," "Coming-to-the-Rescue Literature" and "Hack Literature"[2] are unable to encompass the whole of Chinese literature.

For the purposes of this book, I will divide Chinese literature into four categories: court, scholastic, urban and rural literature. These categories have the merits of directing the reader's attention to the different subject matter and content of each of the four types and at the same time taking into account the physical environment which gave birth to and nurtured literary works, as well as their writers and those who appreciated them.

9   Court literature

What do we mean by court literature? Basically it is writing which has the courts of emperors and kings at its center, and where were gathered groups of literati whose creative works described the tranquil and embellished life of the court and sang its praises. There are three standards for concretely measuring court literature:

1   The scene of the action is necessarily a royal or imperial court. The monarch should be either a literary man himself or one who sets great store by the civil administration and the patronage of scholars. The ruler should gather around him a coterie of literati, treat them lavishly and encourage their literary creation. The scholars, in turn, should serve as the monarch's advisors, teachers or supporters, and in any case should advance their creative works in harmony with the ruler's tastes.
2   The work should be the creation of a scholar. The court Music Bureau was the government office responsible for the collection and performance of folk songs and ballads, but the Music Bureau was not the source of court literature.
3   The literary works which were produced at an imperial or royal court tended to have an overall similar style. They formed a school or orthodoxy, and had a comparatively great influence on the literary creativity of their time.

In the history of Chinese literature, the essence of court literature can be illustrated by the few examples below:

Emperors Wu and Xuan of the Western Han Dynasty

During the rule of Emperor Wu, Western Han reached the peak of its prosperity. Thanks to his encouragement and patronage there gathered at his court a group of officials who excelled at writing *ci* and *fu* poetry. They included Sima Xiangru, Mei Gao and Dongfang Shuo. Emperor Xuan's court boasted Wang Bao and Liu Xiang, among others. Ban Gu, in his "Preface to the Fu Poetry of Two Capitals," says: "In the times of Wu and Xuan court officials skilled in language, such as Sima Xiangru, Yuqiu Shouwang, Dongfang Shuo, Mei Gao, Wang Bao and Liu Xiang discussed and exchanged ideas day and night; senior court officials such as

Ni Kuan, Kong Zang, Dong Zhongshu, Liu De and Crown Prince Xiao Wangzhi composed poems and exchanged them with each other . . . so that by the time of Emperor Xiaocheng over 1,000 such poems had been recorded.[3]

These works elaborate grandly on life in the capital, in the palaces and on the hunting field. They laud the prosperity of the empire and extol the authority of the emperor. So it is no wonder that the emperors had great affection for them. In the *History of the Han Dynasty * Biography of Mei Gao* it says:

> It was because of his *fu* compositions that Mei Gao attracted the emperor's favor and was installed in a palace position. He was ordered to write a *fu* poem about the Pingle [Pacification of the East] Hall, which he did magnificently. For this he was promoted to court gentleman and sent as an envoy to the Xiongnu nomads. Mei Gao was not well versed in the Confucian classics, and he scoffed at the formal rules of poetry. His *fu* poems were often frivolous, and for that he often came under opprobrium.[4]

The *History of the Han Dynasty * Biography of Wang Bao* says:

> Emperor Xuan ordered that Wang Bao and Zhang Ziqiao be on call at any moment. Many a time, he allowed Wang Bao and others to join his large-scale safaris. Whenever they came to a palace or a manor, the emperor would ask them to write poems and sing songs. Then he passed judgment on their works and rewarded them according to their merits. His councilors mostly thought of the activities as extravagant and frivolous. Emperor Xuan retorted, "What about chess playing? Isn't it an elegant pursuit to play chess when at our leisure? The masterpieces of their rhymed compositions can be as significant as classic poems. Besides, they are also full of witty argumentation and pleasant rhetorical language. Among textiles and embroidered fabrics, there are silk and satin; among various pieces of music, there are the folksongs of Zheng and Wei, which the common people still find entertaining. Compared with the folksongs, the literary works in question are replete with righteous significance and allegorical references that make us more observant of the natural world embracing birds, animals, grass and trees. They are far superior to chess games played by artisans." Before long, Emperor Xuan promoted Wang Bao to Grand Master for Remonstration.[5]

From the above two passages, we can see that Emperors Wu and Xuan offered rewards for the composition of *ci* and *fu* poems. We can also discern how *ci* and *fu* poems flourished as court literature.

Emperor Jianwen of Ling and the Later Master of Chen

This was the time when "palace-style poetry" took center stage. The term "palace style" was coined at the court of Xiao Gang, Emperor Jianwen of Liang (reign: 550–552). In the *History of the Liang Dynasty * Biography of Emperor Jianwen* it says: "In the preface to his copy of the *Book of Odes*, the emperor says, 'I became addicted to poetry at the age of seven, and as I became older I did not tire of it.' But the poetry of his time became light and frivolous, and gained the epithet 'palace style.'"[6] According to the *History of the Southern Dynasties * Biography of Xu Chi*, it was Xu Chi who was responsible for this style: "It was felt that a new way of composition was needed, one that shook off the trammels of the old, stale forms. *Chunfang* (people in the crown prince's palace) studied Xu Chi's poetic method, and gave it the name 'palace style,'[7] and so it dates from the period of the court of Emperor Jianwen, and was the poetic form used to describe the main events of court life. The overall tone is a frivolous one."

In the *History of the Sui Dynasty * Record of Classics and Documents* it says: "When Emperor Jianwen of Liang was in the Eastern Palace [i.e., when he was crown prince] he was fond of literature, delighting in lucid words and fine composition, stopping reading only to sleep. The style which he favored – and was therefore imitated both at the court and outside it – was an ornate one the subject matter of which was confined to the doings in the palace chambers. It came to be called the 'palace style.'"[8] Representative of "palace-style poetry" are some of the poems included by Xu Chi's son, Xu Ling, in the *New Recitals from the Jade Terrace*.[9]

We can get a glimpse of conditions at the court of the Later Master of Chen from the *History of the Southern Dynasties * Biography of the Later Master of Chen*:

> Indulging himself in wine and women, Houzhu of Chen neglected state affairs. . . . He often sat among his wives Zhang and Chen as well as six imperial concubines. He often invited ten of his intimate ministers including Jiang Zong and Kong Fan to accompany him at his lavish dinners. Each time he would start by asking the eight ladies to fold paper and write on it poems they were to compose with five characters to a line. He also required that the ten male guests chime in with their own verses. The one who came up with his work the latest would be made to drink as a forfeit. The emperor and his subjects then drank to their hearts' content day in and day out. This practice became the order of the day.[10]

Let us glance at the poem "A Beauty Looks at a Painting" by Xiao Gang, Emperor Jianwen of Liang:

> The goddesses in the paintings,
> And the beauties in the court hall,
> Alas, they are all but pictures, and
> Who can tell one from the other?
> All share the same sparkling eyes;
> All have the same graceful shapes.
> Only the presence of vitality.
> Can set the two groups apart.[11]

Tang Emperors Taizong, Gaozong and Zhongzong and Empress Wu

During his reign, Emperor Taizong established the Ministry of Literature and the Hall of Grand Letters. He also invited scholars to recite poetry. Famous court poets of this era were Yu Shinan, Ouyang Xu, Li Baiyao, Li Yifu and Shangguan Yi. Taizong had the intention of turning literature in a new direction. In his "Preface to Writings of the Imperial Capital," he says,

> Abandoning the substantial to go after the superficial,
> Following the same desires as mankind,
> Bringing confusion to the Great Way,
> Are what a gentleman considers shameful.

In the same poem, he says, "You can enjoy elegant sounds/Only when the ditties of Zheng and Wei have been abandoned."[12] But in the end he did not succeed in turning literature in a new direction, for what he wrote were simply "palace-style poems," and the Liang and Chen styles predominated at his court. Of course, being a ruler, he would desire such an ornamental and tranquil form of literature to grace his court. In his "Holding Court on the First Day of the Year" Emperor Taizong had the collaboration of famous poets such as Wei Zheng, Cen Wenben, Yang Shidao and Li Baiyao. And in his "Gazing at the Sea on a Spring Day" he had the help of Yang Shidao and Xu Jingzong. Most of the surviving poems of Yang Shidao, Xu Jingzong, Yu Shinan and Shangguan Yi echo each other. Shangguan Yi was the most famous of these poets. Having scored top of the civil service examination in the Zhenguan reign period (627–650) of Emperor Taizong, he was appointed by the emperor an academician of the Hall of Grand Letters. At every banquet and official function Shangguan Yi recited his poems for the entertainment of the gathering. "Elegant and polished," his poems had many imitators; in fact, the people of the time called his style the "Shangguan style."

In the reigns of the emperors Gaozong and Zhongzong and that of Empress Wu recitals of *fu* poems by both sovereigns and officials as entertainment at banquets were very much in vogue. Leading poets of the time were Li Jiao, Shen Quanqi and Song Zhiwen. The *Records of Tang Poetry* says: "On the last day of the first lunar month of the reign of Emperor Zhongzong, His Majesty made an excursion to Kunming Lake to enjoy a poetry recital. His officials composed over 100 poems at the emperor's direction. Enthroned in the gaudy pavilion in front of the main hall, he ordered Zhao Rong [a title] to choose a suitable new tune. The officials gathered below His Majesty, and in an instant were scribbling away furiously, each wishing to make a name for himself."[13]

This Zhao Rong was the granddaughter of Shangguan Yi, and her name was Wan'er. She had been received into the palace by Empress Wu. After Emperor Zhongzong came to the throne she was promoted to the position of Zhao Rong, "[Wan'er] persuaded the emperor to expand the academy, increase the enrollment of academicians, and invite ministers and famed scholars to compete for candidacy. Many a time did Wan'er invite the ministers to compose poems, and each time she would write a number of them in a row on behalf of the emperor and the empress consort as well as Princesses Changning and Changle. She also rewarded the ministers with wine in accordance with their merits during poetry contests. Writing poems in the court thus became a trend. The poems composed by the ministers at that time might have been mostly flashy and frivolous, but their sheer number was striking. Therefore the proliferation of poems should be accredited to Wan'er."[14] Thus one can imagine the situation of court literature at the time. This tradition of one person writing a poem to which one or more others reply using the same rhyme sequence lasted till the reign of the Tang Emperor Xuan, though the mainstream of poetry had already shifted outside the court. The discussion of the shift, however, will be omitted here.

Let us look at two lines from the *ci* poem "Lofty Aspiration" by Li Yifu: "Feebly she's folding up her lover's quilt; Lifting the bed curtains, she blushes still. Like him lavish in tenderness last night, Now a spring breeze sneaks in for a tryst."[15]

An alternative title for this poem, "To a Beautiful Woman," has a whiff of the "palace style" of the Liang and Chen courts, as does Shangguan Wan'er's "Poem dedicated on the Occasion of the Emperor's Visit to the Xinfeng Spa Palace":

> In the third winter of the Jinglong reign period,
> A procession of splendid carriages,
> Visited the scenic Ba River.
> Pulled ahead by glittering dragons, not horses,
> Looking back, the frosty fields have turned to pure jade.

This poem was written by Shangguan Wan'er on the 12th day of the 12th (lunar) month of the third year (709) of the Jinglong reign period, when Tang Emperor Zhongzong paid a visit to the Xinfeng Spa Palace. The language used exudes an elegant and refined spirit.[16]

Other types of court poetry which emerged after the Tang Dynasty are worth mentioning – for instance, that written by the group of 17 poets who formed the "Western Kun Style" in the reigns of the Song emperors Taizong and Zhenzong. The leading figures of this school were Yang Yi, Liu Yun and Qian Weiyan, whose works were collected in the *Anthology of Poetic Responses of the Western Kun School*. In the preface to this work, Yang Yi says, "Having been honored with the task of helping to edit this book, I found that I had to follow the trends of thought of the masters celebrated in it. . . . Perusing in sequence posthumous writings, it is necessary to cast an eye over previous works, draw from them their fragrance, bring out their freshness, present their melodies in a new format and let them sharpen each other."[17] These men were all court officials, but in their free time, when they were not drafting official decrees and editing documents, they would entertain each other by writing poems, which the other would strive to match. The contents of these poems would be lyrical or erotic, or would be stories of the courts of previous rulers. The thoughts of love in Mi Yan's poems led to the latter being called "Mi Yan poetry," and he himself claimed to have studied the works of Li Shangyin. In the Ming Dynasty too, especially during the reigns of Emperors Yongle and Hongzhen, court poetry was written in the so-called "Terrace and Pavilion Style" by poets represented by Yang Shiqi, Yang Rong and Yang Pu. They were all accomplished scholars and wrote large numbers of poems at imperial behest. The contents of their poems extolled palace life, and the language is carefree and relaxed, refined and elegant.

Court literature represented the artistic tastes of the highest class of society in feudal China. These works had a tremendous influence in those days, but not many have withstood the test of time. Court literature did, however, contribute something to the development of Chinese literature from the aspects of form and technique. The efforts of the court poets are not unconnected with the rise of the *fu* form of poetry, and the maturity of the techniques of modern poetry in the aspects of antithesis, intonation and use of allusion.

Notes

1 *Collected Writings of Nan Lei*, Vol. 2, "A Written Request to Lord Zhang for Compiling the County Annals", *Collected Writings of the Four Basic Branches of Literature*
2 "Literature that Helps or Decorates" in *An Addendum to Collections Out of Collections*. See *The Collected Works of Lu Xun*, Vol. 7, People's Literature Publishing House, 1973, P. 783
3 Li Shan, Lu Yan et al. [Tang Dynasty]: *Selection of the Literary Works of Six Officials*, Vol. 1, *Collected Writings of the Four Basic Branches of Literature*
4 Ban Gu [Han Dynasty]: *History of the Han Dynasty*, Vol. 51, Zhonghua Book Company, 1962, P. 2366
5 Ban Gu [Han Dynasty]: *History of the Han Dynasty*, Vol. 64, Part 2 Zhonghua Book Company, 1962, P. 2829
6 Yao Silian [Tang Dynasty]: *History of the Liang Dynasty*, Vol. 4, Zhonghua Book Company, 1973, P. 109
7 Li Yanshou [Tang Dynasty]: *History of the Southern Dynasties*, Vol. 62, Zhonghua Book Company, 1973, P. 1521
8 Wei Zheng et al. [Wei Zheng et al.]: *History of the Sui Dynasty*, Vol. 35, Zhonghua Book Company, 1973, P. 1090
9 Xu Ling ed. [Chen Dynasty]: *New Chants From the Jade Terrace*, Vol. 10, reprint of the Song Dynasty original by the Xiaowan Company of Mr. Zhao of Mount Minghan
10 Li Yanshou [Tang Dynasty]: *History of the Southern Dynasties*, Vol. 10, P. 306
11 Xu Ling ed. [Chen Dynasty]: *New Chants From the Jade Terrace*, Vol. 7, reprint of the Song Dynasty original by the Xiaowan Company of Mr. Zhao of Mount Minghan
12 *Complete Tang Poems*, Vol.1, Zhonghua Book Company, 1960, P. 1
13 Ji Yougong [Song Dynasty]: *Records of Tang Poetry*, Vol.3, "Zhao Rong Gains Office" section, *Collected Writings of the Four Basic Branches of Literature*
14 Ouyang Xiu and Song Qi [Song Dynasty]: *A New History of the Tang Dynasty*, Vol. 76, *The First Half of the Queens and Maids * A Biography of Shangguan Zhaorong With a Biography of Empress Wei Attached*, Zhonghua Book Company, 1965, P. 3488
15 *Complete Tang Poems*, Vol. 35, Zhonghua Book Company, 1960, P. 468
16 *Complete Tang Poems*, Vol. 5, Zhonghua Book Company, 1960, P. 61
17 Yang Yi [Song Dynasty]: "Introduction to the Collection of Response Poems of Xi Kun", *Collected Writings of the Four Basic Branches of Literature*

10 Scholastic literature

The term "scholastic" is first found in the *Annals of the Three Kingdoms* Biographies of Wu Zhi and Lu Su*: "They rode in gaudy carriages, associated with officials and hobnobbed with members of the scholastic world." In his "Proclamation Issued in Yuzhou for Yuan Shao," Chen Kongzhang (Lin) says, "This has caused anguish among the scholars and resentment among the people."[1] The term meant a gathering of literary figures, and was somewhat equivalent to today's "intellectuals." The first character, "shi," was a general designation for government officials. A person of excellent learning was also called a "shi." However, very few such people could devote themselves completely to writing; the majority enjoyed an official position. Therefore, "scholastic circles" could also be understood as "official circles." Some officials indeed did serve the emperor himself as literary adjutants, and others were originally low-ranking but rose by virtue of their literary skills coming to the attention of the emperor. Both types of people belonged to the "scholastic" ranks. As I have already discussed the "court literati" in previous chapters, I will next deal with intellectuals who wrote popular works about town life.

"Scholastic literature" was an important part of literary creativity in ancient China. Its content is quite rich and heterogeneous, but it can be roughly divided into the following categories:

Concern for the country and the people, allegorical mourning for the times

This category involved the expression of opinion about the current state of governance, the rise and fall of the country and the sufferings of the people. Such opinions tended to be expressed allegorically with the intention of promoting political reform. Examples are Du Fu's "Song of the Conscripts," "A Beauty Passes," "A 500-word Song of Aspiration Written on My Way to Fengxian County from the Capital" and "The North Expedition"; Bai Juyi's "Songs of Qinzhong" and "New Yuefu Poems"; Liu Zongyuan's "On the Snake-catcher"; Mei Yaochen's "Words of the Peasant Family" and Fan Chengda's "Fan Chengda's "Pressing for Payment of Land Rent." Let us take a look at Du Fu's "Spring View":

On war-torn land streams flow and mountains stand,
In towns spring grass and bushes run riot.

> Grieved over the years, flowers shed tears,
> Seeing us part, the very birds lament.
> Beacon fires have blazed for three months now,
> Letters from home are worth their weight in gold.
> I scratch my grey head and feel the thinning hair,
> Too thin to hold a mere hairpin.[2]

This poem was written in the third month of the second year (757) of the Zhide reign period of Tang Emperor Suzong. At that time the capital, Chang'an, was occupied by the rebel troops of An Lushan. Du Fu was in Chang'an at that time, and he was obsessed with worry about the country, mourned for the times and was constantly thinking of his family. It is reminiscent of Bai Juyi's "Red-threaded Carpet," the short introduction to which speaks of the "nibbling away of mulberry leaves by the silkworms." The allegory here rests on the silk carpets sent as local tribute by the magistrate of Xuanzhou every year for the enjoyment of the imperial court, but which wasted both human and material resources.

> Does the magistrate of the city of Xuan know or not?
> One stretch of carpet needs a thousand double threads.
> The ground does not know that a cold man needs warmth,
> Rare indeed when a man's garments clothe the ground![3]

This poem was written to express indignation at official extravagance. The poet's wrath clearly boils over in the words he uses.

Under the influence of Confucian doctrine, many Chinese scholars and officials came to harbor the ambition to "cultivate the self, put their family in order, govern the country and make the world peaceful." They made positive efforts to engage with society, eager to rescue the common people from their sufferings and guide the country to a situation of tranquility. In his "A Letter of Twenty-two Rhymed Lines Respectfully Dedicated to Mr. Wei, Assistant Director of the Left in the Department of State Affairs," Du Fu says, "A polished gentleman, worthy to rank with Yao and Shun, and who yet respects ordinary folk customs."[4] In his "A 500-word Song of Aspiration Written on My Way to Fengxian County from the Capital," he says, "Concerned with the common folks all year round, he sighed and grieved until his blood was boiling."[5] This is an expression of this kind of thought. It does not mean that such poets did not connect their honors and wealth with their individual merits, but they considered that their individual honors and wealth were earned by practicing this ideal. As Cao Zhi said, "Work hard for the state and the people so as to make lasting achievements worthy of being inscribed on monuments of stone or metal."[6] Xin Qiji chimes in with "I want to address His Majesty's state concerns, To win honor in this and the next world."[7] There were also those who refrained from taking credit for their meritorious deeds, such as Li Bai, who said, "I would like to use all my talents to assist you in reining in everything under the sun and unifying the domain of Tang. Once I have accomplished my service to Your Majesty and won honor for my family, I will roam around the world like Fan Li and Zhang Liang. All that can be done with ease."[8] This ideological trend of engaging with the world as part of literary theory finds its expression in the words of Bai Juyi: "Just as prose works are written for the times, so too are poems composed for events."[9] He also said, "Our poetic voice we want the monarch to hear, as it stems from the pains of the common people."[10] This meant consciously using literary creation to achieve one's own political objective. Even the "great *fu*" of the Han Dynasty, despite its main theme being the eulogizing of achievements and virtues, contained some allegorical meaning.

Care for the fate of the country, care for the sufferings of the people, care for governance and care for reality, stepping high and broadening the vision: These were all parts of the fine tradition of scholastic literature, which deserved to be developed and promoted.

Describing from the heart one's encounters with misfortune

The chief way for some poets to describe their feelings upon encountering misfortune in political life, and to express their ideals and personalities, was to relate historical incidents in verse. Examples are Ruan Ji's "Chanted from the Heart," Zuo Si's "Singing of History," Tao Yuanming's "Song of the Poor Scholar," Chen Zi'ang's "Disappointment" and a poem by Zhang Jiuling with the same title. Besides these there are many other literary works which, although they do not have "disappointment," "chanting from the heart" or "singing of history" as their themes, are nevertheless poems or essays describing political conditions. Examples are Chen Zi'ang's "Upon Mounting Youzhou Tower," Li Bai's "Thoughts on Drinking Alone on a Cold Night," Liu Yuxi's "Reply to Bai Juyi Whom I Met for the First Time at a Banquet in Yangzhou," Lu You's "Just Clearing up after Spring Rain in Lin'an" and "Writing of Indignation," Wen Tianxiang's "Healthy Atmosphere," Gong Zizhen's "Miscellaneous Poems of Ji Hai" ("Violent Storm in the Jiuzhou Islands") and Han Yu's four "Miscellaneous Discourses." Qu Yuan's "Li Sao" and "Nine Pieces" also belong to this category, which contains a large number of poems that give penetrating insights into their authors' innermost feelings. Let us take a look at Zuo Si's "Singing of History":

Jing Ke drank in the capital of Yan,
To his content, his spirits were high.
To Jianli's zither he sang in sorrow,
As if there were no on-lookers.
Jing may have failed in his mission;
But his deed still no one can match.
Looking on the world as he was,
He despised the rich and powerful.
The rich saw themselves as great,
To him they were but useless dust.
Some may consider him a low hero,
But he proved to be a heavy weight.[11]

This poem describes the disdain felt by a poor scholar for a rich aristocrat, and the former's lofty character, which spurns the vulgar fashions of the times. The two characters which mean "humble wretch" form the acme of the meaning of the verses. Similar is Zhang Xiaoxiang's "Niannujiao (Remembering a Beauty) – Crossing Dongting Lake":

> Lake Dongting, Lake Green Grass,
> Near the Mid-Autumn night,
> Unruffled for no winds pass.
> Like thirty thousand acres of jade bright,
> Dotted with the leaf like boat of mine.
> The skies with clear moonbeams overflow,
> The water surface paved with moonlight,
> Brightness above, brightness below.
> My heart with the moon becomes one,
> Felicity to share with none.
>
> Thinking of the southwest, where I spent a year,
> To lonely, pure moonlight akin,
> I feel my heart and soul snow- and ice-clear.
> Although my hair is sparse, my gown too thin,
> In the immense expanse I keep floating up.
> Drinking wine from the River West,
> And using the Dipper as a cup,
> I invite Nature to be my guest.
> Beating time on the boat and crooning alone,
> I sink deep into time and place unknown.[12]

The poet has resigned from office because of slander, and as he crosses Dongting Lake on his journey he writes this poem. The words he uses describe the local scenery, but their hidden intent is to express the lofty character and noble aspirations of the poet himself. The verse "Brightness above, brightness below" not only describes the nocturnal scenery of Dongting Lake, it also describes the poet's own bright and open-minded nature." In the immense expanse I keep floating up" is a display of brimming self-confidence, and the lines "Drinking wine from the River West/And using the Dipper as a cup/I invite Nature to be my guest" represent his daring soul.

The importance attached by Chinese scholar-officials to individual inquiry lay in the problems of "chu" [provenance] and "chu" [location], and "qiong" and "da." It was said that "da" was universal goodness while "qiong" was the goodness of a single person.[13] These two combined to form a universal attitude to human life. It was the ideological contradictions and fluctuations of feeling which arose from these two questions that formed the main content of literary works. The "feelings," "misfortune" and "heart" in the "heartfelt singing of feelings of misfortune" overwhelmingly stemmed from the course of the different types of psychological and emotional activities sparked by the contrasts between those two opposites. A simpler way of putting it would be to define it as the contradiction between ideology and reality and between the individual and society. The scholar-officials all harbored their own aspirations and had a certain amount of skill and knowledge, but, stifled by the power relations at that time they felt out of tune with the times and despaired of using their talents to the full. Therefore, they took up the writing brush to express their anguish and attack the rich and powerful. Such expressions as "The poor scholar loses his post and his ambition is thwarted,"[14] and "He pours out his troubles in verse"[15] embrace this very idea, and encapsulate the content of literary works of the "heartfelt singing of feelings of misfortune" genre.

Landscape and pastoral lyrics

Landscape and pastoral themes of literature are often conflated, but there is a real distinction between the two. The first takes mountain and streams, i.e., the natural scenery, as the principal objects of description, while the latter focuses on the life of the recluse amid fields and gardens. Landscape and pastoral works often comprise a combination of journeying, the leaving of home to take up an official position, seclusion, search for immortals, etc. Examples are Cao Cao's "Viewing the Boundless Sea," Xie Lingyun's "Entering the Outlet of Lake Pengli," Tao Yuanming's "Returning to Dwell in the Country," Wang Wei's "A View of the River Han," Li Bai's "Gazing at the Waterfall on Mount Lu," Du Fu's "Gazing at Mount Tai," Liu Zongyuan's "Eight Records of Yongzhou," Su Shi's "Verses on the Red Cliff," Yuan Chengda's "Miscellaneous Joys of the Four Seasons in the Country" and Zhang Dai's "Watching the Snow from a Lake Pavilion." Let us take a look at the chapter of "Commentary on River Water" of Li Daoyuan's *Commentary on the Waterways Classic*:

Seven hundred *li* (a *li* is about 0.3 of a mile) from the Three Gorges, the Yangtze River is flanked by rolling mountains that seldom break. Peaks rising one after another blot out the sky and the sun. Naturally the sunshine and the moonlight are not visible until noon and midnight. River traffic is impossible in the summer, when the Yangtze River swells up to inundate the hilly areas. Sometimes, at an urgent call from the monarch, one starts off at Baidi and reaches Jiangling at dusk, covering a distance of 1,200 *li*. Though with the wind, speed is still hard to pick up. During spring and winter the water becomes clear where it is shallow and green where it is deep, giving reflections of whatever lies on both sides. The precipices, from which waterfalls cascade downward, host grotesquely shaped fir trees. Coupled with the exuberance of the vegetation, the scenery is all the more intriguing. Whenever it clears up or the morning sets in with frost, long screeches of monkeys can be heard coming from the cold forests interspersed with cool springs. Sounding sorrowful in the hollow valleys, their whoops echo into the far distance. As fishermen often sing, "Wu stretches the longest of the Three Gorges in Sichuan; only three screeches of the monkeys there will cause you to cry."[16]

The first seven verses describe the mountains; the next eight describe the river. From "During spring and winter" to "the scenery is all the more intriguing" the description includes both. There is a special charm in how the mountains are reflected in the water and how the waterfall leaps from the mountainside. The description then goes on to deal with the traveller's feelings, and the lingering echo of the fisherman's song at the conclusion leaves a pleasant aftertaste. Similar is the poem "Mountain Eternal South" by Wang Wei:

> The highest peak scrapes the sky blue;
> It extends from hill to sea.
> When I look back, clouds shut out the view;
> When I come near, no mist I see.
> Peaks vary on the north and south sides;
> Vales differ in sunshine and shade.
> Seeking a lodge where to abide;
> I ask a woodman when I wade.[17]

The first six verses express what the poet sees, while the last two verses deal with his feelings as he picks up his writing brush to describe the magnificence of The Southernmost Mountain. This is similar to Yuan Zhongdao's "On Visiting Mount Jun," which combines depictions of scenery with descriptions of lyricism. The last part of this poem goes like this:

> Towards the evening, we went back to the mountain pass, found a crag to sit on, and started enjoying the view of the transformations of the misty clouds above Lake Dongting. I said to Wang Zhangfu: "Normally only the clouds in summer are peculiar, and the ones above this lake are more so. Spreading as far as 800 *li*, these vapors rise hazily and sparklingly into the air, creating all kinds of forms one can find in the world or any image a sculptor can shape with uncanny craftsmanship. It turns out that this fantastic view on Lake Dongting is perhaps what Mi Fu once told us about the scenery from which he drew the inspiration for his paintings. How can I find a hut in the bamboo forest to settle down so that I can enjoy the sounds, and the views of the misty clouds in my late years?" That night, Wang Zhangfu was seized with a desire to find a location here to build his residence. The mists above the lake became chilly, and we found it hard to go to sleep. The next morning, gusts of wind sprang up. We hurried away from the sacred mountain and sailed down to beneath the Yueyang Tower.[18]

Again, in Yuan Chengda's "Miscellaneous Joys of the Four Seasons in the Country":

> Newly made earthen grounds are as plain as mirrors,
> Every family is busy threshing on frost-free days.

Laughter and songs rise and fall like thunder,
Amidst the sound of flailing all through the night.[19]

This is a pastoral poem describing the scene on the threshing ground at the time of the autumn harvest in a very lively and appealing way.

Nature is a very important entity for sparking the literary imagination. The works of the scholar-officials are full of interest and emotion when they write about the mountains, streams, grass, trees, sun, moon and stars that make up the natural world, the natural environment which humans rely on for their existence. The scholar-officials sing of nature, personify natural scenery, instilling their own thoughts and feelings into it, and make nature the most prominent theme of scholar-official literature. Lu Ji, in his "Rhapsody on Literature," says, "Encompassing the whole universe, with the myriad things sitting on the tip of the writing brush."[20] Liu Xie, in his *Carving a Dragon with a Literary Heart * The Physical World*, says, "Spring and autumn roll around, succeeding one another, and the *yin* and *yang* principles alternatingly darken and brighten. When objects in the physical world change, our minds are also affected."[21] Zhong Rong, in his "Preface to Poetical Works," says, "The spirit that moves things, the objects that stir up the feelings . . . These are what stimulate the emotions and take shape in the form of song and dance . . . For moving Heaven and Earth and putting man in touch with the spirit world nothing approaches poetry."[22] From these representative passages we can see what an important place the relationship between man and nature occupies in literary creation. In the realm of poetry and ballad alone, we do not find many works that directly express the author's innermost feelings without borrowing imagery from the outside world. And most of these images are taken from nature. We could even say that if images from the natural world were removed, there would be no Chinese poetry. We can even go one step further and say that Chinese scholar-official literature is built on harmony between the natural world and man, and therefore the sublime realm of literature lies in the interchanges between man and the natural world.

If we go a step further in our inquiry into the origin of this, we cannot help but investigate the literary psychology of the Chinese people. The Chinese recognize man as a part of nature, and pursue harmony with nature in a state called "Heaven and man are one." The highest ideal of human life is to consciously reach the realm where "Heaven and man are one." With this ideological premise, it is necessary to adopt an attitude that accommodates the natural world. At the same time, the relationship between man and nature becomes a major theme of scholar-official literature, and this relationship is displayed as a special one.

Frontier journeys

As early as in the Han Dynasty, works depicting the life of expeditionary soldiers appeared, with the Music Bureau's "South of the Embattled City." In the periods of the Wei, Jin and Southern and Northern Dynasties literary men studied the Music

Bureau poems and produced a steady stream of works dealing with frontier journeys. A noted one of these is Bao Zhao's "Modeled After 'Coming out of the North Gate of Ji City'" (Note: Many poems of this period had no proper title, and they are identified by the tune to which they were chanted.) In the Tang Dynasty it was common for literary men to enlist in the army to experience frontier life. "I'd rather fight at a hundred men's head; Than pore o'er books without performing feats"[23] was a widespread way of thinking at that time. Some of the frontier poems of the Tang Dynasty discuss the pros and cons of frontier defense from a politician's point of view, like Gao Shi's "Song of the Northern Frontier"; some described the outlandish scenery of the frontier through a poet's eyes, like Cen Shen's "Seeing off Magistrate Wu on His Way Back to the Capital in the Snow" and "Song of Running Horse River"; and some deal with the mixed feelings of soldiers who are determined to serve their country but miss their homes, like Wang Changling's "I Would Rather Fight" and "On the Frontier." Besides these, Wang Zhihuan, Li Qi, Wang Wei, Li Bai, Du Fu and Li Yi all wrote poems of frontier life. Among the Song Dynasty *ci* poems which treat of frontier garrison life, the most famous are Fan Zhongyan's "Yujiaao (Pride of Fishermen)" and Xin Qiji's "Pozhenzi (Breaking a Military Formation): A *Ci* Poem of Heroism as a Message to Chen Tongfu." Let us take a look at Gao Shi's "Song of the Northern Frontier":

A cloud of smoke and dust spreads o'er the northeast frontier.
To fight the remnant foe, our generals leave the rear.
Brave men should go no matter where.
The emperor bestows on them his favor.
To the sound of drum and gong to Elm Pass.
Round Mount Stone Tablet flags flutter.
Urgent orders speed over the Sea of Sand.
The enemy has set Mount Wolf aflame.
The border hills and streams are desolate.
Enemy horsemen lash us like wind and rain.
Half our men lied dead on the battleground.
While pretty girls in camp still sing and dance.
Scrub withers in the lingering autumn.
At sunset few are the city gate guards.
Trusting the emperor, they scorn the foe.
The city is under siege, they know.
Armored they keep a watch on the frontier.
Their wives have shed streams of tears.
In southern towns the broken-hearted women weep.
In vain their men look southward, still far apart.
With the northern front at stake, how can they leave?
On the border vast and desolate, how can they stay?
All day the slaughter threatens again and again.
At night the clang of gong echoes o'er the plain.
Both sides' swords are stained with blood.
What reward is worth surrendering life?

Do you not know? The bitter strife with the foe.
The general too should share their weal and woe.[24]

This poem contains descriptions of the hardships of active service for the ordinary soldier and how he and his loved ones at home miss each other. It also describes how the officers neglect the men's welfare and even on campaign hanker after enjoyment and luxuries. The short introduction to the poem reads: "In the 26th year (738) of the Kaiyuan reign period I accompanied the imperial historian Zhang Gong on an expedition to the border and back. I describe this in my 'Song of the Northern Frontier.' My feelings about life defending the frontier are all contained in it." Although this poem clearly deals with feelings and impressions related to the soldier's life, its content is not limited to the northeastern battlefields but has a much wider significance. There is a political coloration in its concrete and lively description which makes it fully capable of representing a lofty style.

Now let us take a look at Cen Shen's "Seeing off Magistrate Wu on His Way Back to the Capital in the Snow":

Snapping the pallid grass, the northern wind whirls low.
In the eighth moon the Tartar sky is filled with snow.
As if the vernal breeze had come back overnight.
Adorning thousands of pear trees with blossoms white.
Flakes enter pearled blinds and wet the silken screen.
No furs of fox can warm us, nor brocaded quilts green.
The general cannot draw his rigid bow with ease.
Even the commissioner in coat of mail would freeze.
Wilderness ice spreads far and near.
And gloomy clouds hang sad and drear.
We drink to our guest homeward bound.
With Tarter lutes and pipes the camps resound.
Snow in large flakes covers the camp gate.
The frozen flag resists the windy spate.
At the Wheel Tower's eastern gate we bid goodbye.
On the snow-covered road to the Heavenly Mountains high.
I watch as he rounds a bend and is lost to sight.
His horse's tracks will soon be covered by the snow in flight.[25]

The entire poem consists of 18 stanzas. The first 10 are descriptions of the snow; it is only in the 11th that we come to the parting. The snow is only the background to the parting, but the poet puts a great deal of effort into elaborating on it. His motivation for this is to convey to his countrymen the beauty and attraction of the frontier of their native land, despite the coldness of the climate and the harsh conditions for existence there. The clever and original analogy contained in the stanzas "As if the vernal breeze had come back overnight/Adorning thousands of pear trees with blossoms white," with its natural and fluent wording, reaches the acme of poetic perfection.

Fan Zhongyan's poem to the tune "Pride of Fishermen" is a fine example of a *ci* poem with a border theme:

> When autumn comes to the frontier, the scene is drear.
> Southbound wild geese won't stay.
> Even for one day.
> An uproar arises.
> Horns blow far and near.
> Walled in by peaks, smoke rises straight.
> At sunset over town with locked gate.
> I hold wine, yet home is far away.
> The northwest is not yet won.
> Flutes wail with doleful strains.
> Frost covers the ground.
> Sleep comes to none.
> The general's hair turns white.
> And the soldiers weep.[26]

Fan Zhongyan once served as magistrate of Bin County[27] in Shaanxi Province, and so he had personal experience of guarding the frontier. This is what gives this poem such heartfelt appeal.

Literary works as gifts of gratitude and parting

Expressions of friendship were important themes of scholar-official literature. And so there are many works of this genre, as poems and essays were particularly convenient as gifts of gratitude and parting gifts between host and guest. Among poetic works of this type are Tao Yuanming's "Reply to General Pang's Poem," Wang Bo's "Farewell to Prefect Du," Wang Wei's "A Farewell Song," Li Bai's "Parting at a Tavern in Jinling," Xin Qiji's "Hexinlang: As Chen Liang Chimed in, I am Replying with a Rhyme" and Chen Liang's "Farewell to Zhang Demao." Among essays of this type are Tao Hongjing's "A Letter to Xie Zhongshu," Han Yu's "A Foreword to 'A Farewell Poem to Li Yuan Retiring to Pangu'" and Wang Anshi's "A Reply to Sima Guang's Poem." There is a plethora of masterpieces of this genre, but as an example let us look at Tao Yuanming's "A Prefaced Reply to General Pang's Poem":

> I've read the poem you wrote to me again and again, and found it hard to tear myself away from it. Two years have elapsed since we became neighbors, and we have just said goodbye to winter and ushered in the second spring. We have quickly become bosom friends through our sincere and pleasant conversations. As the saying goes, "A good friend is made after a few encounters." But our friendship is far more profound. Unfortunately things do not always turn out the way we wish, and we now have to part. The grievous sighs that the legendary Yang Zi uttered sound all the more meaningful at this moment. Suffering

from illness for a long time, I have already stopped writing poems. I am frail in the first place, and now I am aging with illness. In accordance with the *Rites of Zhou*'s motto "Courtesy demands reciprocity," I have composed this poem for you as a keepsake so that it may give you some solace when you think of me.

> Intimacy does not have to be time-honored,
> Because friendship can be made at first sight,
> My aspiration and interest you appreciate;
> You come to my garden from time to time.
> Our talk is always agreeable and proper;
> And we both love the classics of past sages.
> Occasionally we have jars of wine ready,
> And we drink at leisure and to our heart's content.
> You know I have been a hermit by nature,
> Harboring no desire for an official career.
> Changeful events cannot diminish friendship,
> Frequent correspondence lessens my worries.
> Affinity can reach as far as a thousand miles,
> Despite the barrier of rivers and mountains.
> May you, my dear friend, stay healthy and sound!
> At what time can we see each other once again?[28]

The preface to this poem is in itself a small literary gem, sincere and simple, and deeply moving. The poem not only describes the cordial relations between the two protagonists, it also expresses the feelings of the two after the parting. The two words "qing tong," meaning affection, have a truly deep meaning. Wang Bo's "Farewell to Prefect Du" is a famous poem of a similar kind:

> You'll leave the town walled far and wide
> For mist-veiled land by riverside.
> I feel on parting sad and drear
> For both of us are strangers here.
> If you've a friend who knows your heart,
> Distance can't keep you two apart.
> At crossroads where we bid adieu,
> Do not shed tears as women do.[29]

The wording of this poem is very simple, but the feelings it evokes are profound. The whole mood of the poem emerges from the carefully worded lines, stirring the reader's feelings. The lines "If you've a friend who knows your heart, Distance can't keep you two apart" have a truly romantic ring to them, and encapsulate the message of the poem. Similar is Xin Qiji's *Hexinlang:*

> Toasting goodbye at the rest pavilion by the roadside,
> You are like the admirable Yuanming and Zhuge Liang.

All of a sudden a magpie perched upon a pine tree,
Flicking off the lingering snowflakes from its branch.
Falling upon us it seems to add to our graying hair.
Snow-covered, the landscape is deprived of its life,
Interspersed with nothing but a few plum trees.
Two or three wild geese make it look all the bleaker.
You came as you promised, but you leave too soon.
With sadness I've rushed over to see you off,
Braving the cold weather that freezes the river.
Alas, it was nearly impossible to get across,
Wheels on the impassible road became blocked,
With cold wind sending a chill along my spine.
Why am I feeling so grieved and so sorrowful?
Because I regret letting you go in the first place.
As if I had molded a huge mistake
With all the iron ore in the world.
The whining wail of a flute in the night
Will not, as I wish, tear out my heart.[30]

According to the brief introduction, this poem was written after Xin Qiji had a short meeting with Chen Liang (Tongfu), and the two had to part. At that time, Xin Qiji "was very reluctant to let Chen Tongfu go. He rushed out, trying to catch up with him. When he reached Egret Forest, the snow was deep and the muddy road was slippery so that he could not move on. He then stopped over at Fang Village, where he drank alone, feeling sad all the time. He hated himself for failing to ask Chen Tongfu to stay. At midnight, he put up at the All-Around View Tower Inn by the Lake of Wushi Spring. A flute being played in the next room saddened him all the more. So he composed a *ci* poem to the tune of "Ruyanfei (A Young Swallow Flying)" (another name for "Hexinlang") to express his feelings. Five days later, Chen Tongfu wrote him a letter to ask for his poem. That was exactly what he wanted to do. So he sent this poem over a thousand *li* hoping that his friend would find it entertaining. Both Xin Qiji and Chen Liang were strong advocates for resistance to the Nurchen invaders, who eventually set up the Jin Dynasty in northern China. Both were also poets. This poem uses a series of images to describe the emotional bond between them and how they miss each other when apart. As such, it can be described as a perfect example of the "parting gift" genre of *ci* poems.

Love and marriage and "the traveller thinking of his wife"

These are old themes in Chinese literature, and many works both of folk and of scholar-official literature emerged on these topics. However, some of the poems that deal with love and marriage and "the traveller thinking of his wife" have political sentiments interwoven. In some of them it is difficult to distinguish what the main theme is, and so it seems best to make a rigid line of division between those with political overtones and those which are clearly devoid of them. The latter include Cao Pi's "Song of the Northern Frontier," Li Bai's "A Trader's Wife," Cui Hu's "Written in a Village South of the Capital," Li Zhiyi's "Busuanzi (Song of Divination)" ("I live on the upstream of the Yangtze"), Zhou Bangyan's "Yulouchun (Jade Spring Pavilion)" ("The Peach Stream is rambling along, not to be stopped") and Lu You's "Chaitoufeng (Phoenix Hairpin)." The former includes Cao Zhi's "Seven-paced Lament," Ruan Ji's "Chanted from the Heart" ("In the west there is a beauty") and Zhu Qingyu's "Presented to Zhang Ji of the Thoughts in the Boudoir." In addition, Li Shangyin's "Untitled" poem belongs in the latter class. Although it touches on a wide range of themes there can be no doubt that the four lines of his "Swallow Tower Ode" and the five lines of his "To the Willow" are purely love poems. Let's take a look at Li Bai's "A Trader's Wife":

My forehead covered by my hair cut straight,
I played with flowers plucked before the gate.
On hobbyhorse you came upon the scene.
Around the well we played with plums still green.
We lived, close neighbors, on Riverside Lane.
Carefree and innocent, we children twain.
At fourteen years, when I became your bride,
I'd often turn my bashful face aside.
Hanging my head, I'd look toward the wall,
A thousand times I'd not answer your call.
At fifteen years, when I'd composed my brow,
To mix my dust with yours was my dear vow.
Rather than break faith, you declared you'd die.
Who knew I'd live alone in a tower high?
I was sixteen when you went far away,
Passing the Three Gorges with their sides so grey.
Where ships were wrecked when spring floods ran high,
Where gibbons' wails seemed to come from the sky.
Green moss now grows before our door.
Your footprints, hidden, can be seen no more.
The moss can't be removed, so thick it grows.
And leaves fall early when the west wind blows.
The yellow butterflies in autumn pass,
Two by two over our garden grass.
This sight would break my heart and I'm afraid,
Sitting alone, my rosy cheeks will fade.
Oh, when are you to leave the western land?
Make sure you let me know beforehand.
I'll walk to meet you, and not call it far,
To go to Long Wind Sands if there you are.[31]

This poem describes a woman's feelings, with the scent of everyday life. The emotions are uncomplicated yet deep, and the wording is ordinary yet moving, and extremely touching. Another example is Zhou Bangyan's "Yulouchun":

> The Peach Stream is rambling along, not to be stopped,
> The autumn lotus roots when cut are not to be re-attached.
> In the past I waited for you on Red-railing Bridge,
> Today I'm walking alone on the path of fallen leaves.
> Draped in a veil of mists are mountains uncountable,
> Flying are the wild geese against the fiery sunset.
> Life is like a cloud drifting above a river after rain.
> Departure elicits a feeling akin to trodden petals.[32]

This *ci* poem was written when the poet had been separated from his lover. He returns to his old haunts and reminisces about times gone by. He attempts to write down his boundless emotional stirrings. The poem's structure, which combines multiple shifts and changes with constant flashbacks, very neatly expresses the lingering sorrow associated with such feelings.

Zhu Qingyu's "Presented to Zhang Ji of the Thoughts in the Boudoir" is an example of a poem in which the writer inserts his own social and political views:

> Last night red candles burned bright in the bridal room;
> At dawn the bride will bow to her new parents with the groom.
> She whispers to him after touching up her face:
> "Have I painted my brows with fashionable grace?"[33]

This poem has the alternative title of "To an Examiner on the Eve of the Examination." Zhu Qingyu wrote it just before taking a civil service examination, and dedicated it to Zhang Ji, Court Gentleman of the Bureau of Waterways and Irrigation. The poem is in reality asking if Zhu's literary skill could satisfy the examiner. However, this is not the meaning that the poet directly expresses: He compares himself to a new bride who asks her husband if her eyebrows are painted in accordance with the fashion of the time. But there is no doubt that Zhang Ji understood the implied meaning. In his "Toast to Zhu Qingyu," Zhang Ji says, "A pretty girl all dressed up appeared at Mirror Lake. Though aware of her own beauty, she still appears pensive. The costly silk of the Qi is no longer as valuable as before; For a Lotus-gathering Girl's song is worth a thousand pieces of gold,"[34] expressing high praise for Zhu's literary skill.

The above six categories roughly cover all the themes and contents of China's scholar-official literature. There are some minor genres, such as those which chart the changes of the seasons, lyrics which describe certain objects, dirges and banquet and outings verses. Some of these can be included in the six categories; for instance, some lyrics which describe certain objects contain personal observations on politics and society, and can be slotted into the "misfortune" category. It is not necessary to elaborate on them one by one here.

Notes

1 Li Shan, Lv Yanji et al. [Tang Dynasty]: *Selection of the Major Writings of Six Officials*, Vol. 44, *Collected Writings of the Four Basic Branches of Literature*

2 *Complete Tang Poems*, Vol. 224, Zhonghua Book Company, 1960, P. 2404

3 *Complete Tang Poems*, Vol. 427, Zhonghua Book Company, 1960, P. 4703

4 *Complete Tang Poems*, Vol. 216, Zhonghua Book Company, 1960, P. 2252

5 *Complete Tang Poems*, Vol. 216, Zhonghua Book Company, 1960, P. 2265

6 "A Letter to Yang Dezu", *Selection of the Major Writings of Six Officials*, Vol. 42, *Collected Writings of the Four Basic Branches of Literature*

7 "Pozhenzi: A Ci Poem of Heroism as a Message to Chen Tongfu", Deng Guangming's *An Annotation to a Chronological Compilation of Xin Qiji's Ci Poems*, Vol. 2, Shanghai Ancient Books Publishing House, 1978, P. 204

8 "A Reply to the Letter of Denunciation from Chamberlain Meng on Behalf of Mt. Shou", *Complete Works of Li Taibo* explained by Wang Qi of the Qing Dynasty, Vol. 26, Zhonghua Book Company, 1977, P. 1225

9 "A Letter to Yuan Zhen", *A Compendium of Tang Literature*, Vol. 675, Zhonghua Book Company, 1983, P. 6888

10 "A Message Sent to Tang Qu", *Complete Tang Poems*, Vol. 424, Zhonghua Book Company, 1960, P. 4663

11 Li Shan, Lv Yanji et al. [Tang Dynasty]: *Selection of the Major Writings of Six Officials*, Vol.21, *Collected Writings of the Four Basic Branches of Literature*

12 *A Few Lines by Zhang Xiaoxiang*, Vol. 1, Photocopy of the Song Dynasty edition by the Sheyuan of Mr. Tao

13 *Mencius * Part One of "Exhausting One's Mental Constitution, Commentary on the Thirteen Classics"*, World Bookstore photocopy of the Ruan woodblock print, P. 2765

14 Song Yu [Warring States Period]: *Nine Discussions*, Hong Xingzu *Additional Commentary on the Songs of Chu*, Vol. 8, Zhonghua Book Company, 1983, P. 138

15 Han Yu [Tang Dynasty]: "Preface to Seeing off Meng Jiao": "All that Is Uneven Makes a Noise", *Collected Works of Han Changli*, Vol. 19, *Collected Writings of the Four Basic Branches of Literature*

16 Wang Guowei: *The Annotated Commentary on the Waterways Classic*, Vol. 34, "River Water 2", Shanghai People's Publishing House, 1984, P. 1067. This piece of writing is taken from "Memories of Jingzhou" by Sheng Hongzhi of the Song Dynasty (See *Comprehensive Categories of Art and Literature*, Vol. 7 and *Imperial Readings of the Taiping Era*, Vol. 53)

17 *Complete Tang Poems*, Vol. 126, Zhonghua Book Company, 1960, P. 1277

18 Kexue Studio Collection redacted by Qian Bocheng, Vol. 15, Shanghai Ancient Books Publishing House, 1989, P. 650

19 *Complete Song Poems*, edited by Fu Xuancong et al., Vol. 2268, Peking University Press, 1991, P. 26005

20 Li Shan, Lv Yanji et al. [Tang Dynasty]: *Selection of the Major Writings of Six Officials*, Vol. 17, *Collected Writings of the Four Basic Branches of Literature*

21 Fan Wenlan: *Carving a Dragon With a Literary Heart Annotated*, People's Literature Publishing House, 1978, P. 693

22 Chen Yanjie: *Poems Annotated*, People's Literature Publishing House, 1962, P. 1

23 Yang Jiong [Tang Dynasty]: "I Would Rather Fight", *Complete Tang Poems*, Vol. 50, Zhonghua Book Company, 1960, P. 611

24 Gao Shi [Tang Dynasty]: *Complete Tang Poems*, Vol. 213, Zhonghua Book Company, 1960, P. 2217

25 Chen Tiemin and Hou Zhongyi: *Annotated Works of Cen Shen*, Vol. 2, Shanghai Ancient Books Publishing House, 1981, P. 163

26 Zhou Miji [Song Dynasty]: *A Selection of Outstanding Ci Poems of the Tang and Song Dynasties*, *Collected Writings of the Four Basic Branches of Literature*

27 Tuo Tuo et al. [Yuan Dynasty]: *History of the Song Dynasty*, Vol. 314, *Biography of Fan Zhongyan*, Zhonghua Book Company, 1977, P. 10275

28 Yuan Xingpei: *Collected Works of Tao Yuanming Annotated*, Zhonghua Book Company, 2003, P. 115

29 *Complete Tang Poems*, Vol. 56, Zhonghua Book Company, 1960, P. 676

30 Deng Guangming: *An Annotation to a Chronological Compilation of Xin Qiji's Ci Poems*, Vol. 2, Shanghai Ancient Books Publishing House, 1993, P. 236

31 *Complete Tang Poems*, Vol. 26, Zhonghua Book Company, 1960, P. 359

32 *Collected Works of Zhou Bangyan*, redacted by Wu Zeyu, Vol. 2, Zhonghua Book Company, 1981, P. 58

33 *Complete Tang Poems*, Vol. 515, Zhonghua Book Company, 1960, P. 5892

34 *Complete Tang Poems*, Vol. 386, Zhonghua Book Company, 1960, P. 4362

11 Urban literature

"Urban" is a general term for streets and marketplaces. The term originated quite early. In the brief Foreword to "The White Elm-Flanked Road by the East Gate" of the *Mao Poems*: "The white elm-flanked road by the East Gate is quickly deteriorating in terms of morality. Lord Chen's debauchery has started a custom, where men and women stray from their norm: gathering more often in the streets than before, they sing and dance openly in the marketplace." Here what is meant by urban literature are the literary forms that entertained and were passed down among the ordinary people of the city streets and markets. Li Kaixian of the Ming Dynasty scoured the streets and marketplaces for romantic *ci* poems, which he collected into a book titled, "Introduction to Urban Romantic *Ci* Poems." Xin Xinzi, in his "Commentary on the Novel *Plum in a Golden Vase*," says, "In this novel are transmitted both the everyday talk of the street and markets, but also boudoir gossip. . . ."[1] Both types of conversation are called "'urban." The background to this is the colloquial speech of the romantic *ci* poems and popular novels such as *Plum in a Golden Vase*.

In fact, the so-called urban literature can be traced back as far as some folk ballads collected by the Han Dynasty Music Bureau. "The Orphan" describes the grief of an orphan cast out by his elder brother and sister-in-law; "Yulinlang (Palace Guard)" tells how Hu Ji, a woman who keeps a wine shop, fends off the unwanted attentions of a local bully; "The Eastern Gate" portrays the perilous life of a townsman who is forced to take risks to earn a living. These works are all in verse and circulated in the streets, reflecting the lives, thoughts and feelings of the lower orders. The overwhelming majority of the "Wu Songs" and "Western Tunes" of the folk ballads of the Southern Dynasties Period were street songs. Guo Maoqian, in his *Collected Poems of the Music Bureau*, says, "After crossing the river from Yongjia, it went down to Liang and Chen, and eventually reached the capital Nanjing. That was how the Songs of Wu originated." Also, "The Western Tunes emerged in the area bounded by the cities of Jing, Ying, Fan and Deng."[2] From this we can clearly see that the "Wu Songs" and "Western Tunes" were products of the streets and markets. The "Western Tunes" especially have a particular flavor of the lives of boatmen and wandering merchants.

Urban literature after the mid-Tang period is mostly "shuo-chang" literature, that is, recitation interspersed with singing. Examples of this are the "bianwen" genre of the Tang Dynasty and some popular folk *ci* poetry. Following in this tradition came the prompt-book stories of the Song and Yuan Dynasties, the poetic drama and Southern Opera of the Yuan Dynasty, the neo-prompt-book stories of the Ming Dynasty and the full-length novels of the Ming and Qing Dynasties. It was in the mid-Tang period that urbanization began to spread rapidly, along with a vigorous development of trade. This situation sparked a blossoming of urban-type entertainments. The painting "Qingming Festival on the River" by Zhang Zeduan presents a vivid picture of the bustling street life on both sides of the river that flows through the Song Dynasty capital of Bian (Kaifeng). In Chapter 5 "Folkways" of his *Brilliant Record of the Dream of the Eastern Capital*, Meng Yuanlao describes the urban folk customs of the Song Dynasty: "The population it has is so large that any addition to or deduction from it would make no difference. It is worthy of the name 'Capital of Fille de Joie, Wine, and Medicinal Herbs Including Aromatic Drugs.' Particularly it boasts secluded lanes and alleys replete with various kinds of pleasure houses. They are too numerous to count."[3] The flourishing of urban literature and art in the Song capital at that time is well depicted by the contemporary writer Luo Hua in his *Records of the Chats of a Drunken Old Man*, in which he addresses the following four lines of verse to storytellers: "Bold are beautiful women in the ardent spring of colorful blooms; Ambitious are heroic men in the freezing wind of moonless nights. With their glib tongues they present their dialogues and soliloquies, Sizing up the world to comment on what's right and what's wrong."[4] Here we can appreciate the skill of urban artists. It was in the fertile soil of the entertainment activities and their "shuo-chang" literature of the streets that new forms of poetry different from the orthodox genres sprouted. This urban literature, with its rich and colorful narrative spirit, added new luster to Chinese literature as a whole, and after progressing though the stages of being recorded by artists, and polished and imitated by literary figures throughout the Yuan, Ming and Qing Dynasties, it finally emerged as a splendid array of works.

Urban literature can be divided into five types according to its theme and content:

Love and marriage

This is the most common theme and content of urban literature. In this type of work the main protagonist is often a girl and an object of warm praise; the male protagonist pales by comparison. Love and marriage stories again can be divided into three types:

The first type is the "passionate girl and the heartless swain" type. The heroine of the story boldly defies feudal morality and challenges the feudal powers. She gives all her love and even her life to some young man, who toys with and then abandons her. In other stories she endures humiliation to shoulder all the burden of the duties of a wife, only to find that her husband starts looking elsewhere for happiness as soon as he becomes rich and famous. These works never fail to show sympathy for the heroine, while pouring opprobrium on the faithless young man. Examples are the "prompt-book" novels "Miss Du in Anger Sinks the Jewel

Box" (see *Ordinary Words to Alarm the World*, edited by Feng Menglong of the Ming Dynasty), the Yuan Dynasty drama "Night Rain by the Xiang River (Yang Xianzhi)" and the Song-Yuan southern drama *The Story of the Lute* (*Gao Ming*).

The second type is the "lovers united in wedlock" type. In these works true lovers overcome all kinds of vicissitudes and barriers to finally become man and wife. A particularly fine example is Wang Shifu's *The Western Chamber*; other accomplished works are Bai Pu's *On the Wall and on a Horse* and Shi Hui's "Pavilion for Greeting the Moon." Also belonging here are the "prompt-book" novel *Yu Tangchun in Distress Finds a Husband* (see *Ordinary Words to Alarm the World*) and the "talented scholar and beautiful girl" novel "Two Who Were Made for Each Other," which emerged in the period of the end of the Ming Dynasty and the beginning of the Qing Dynasty and can be found in the "Arranged in Accordance with the Confucian Code of Ethics." Unfortunately, many works of the "talented scholar and beautiful girl" type have stereotyped plots and show little originality. In this genre the heroine is the vehicle for pushing the plot forward. She is depicted as having a fresh personality and completely overshadows her lover. The authors of such works were obviously emotionally inclined toward the heroines.

The third type is the "phantom marriage" type. This describes a metamorphosed marriage in the conditions of fierce feudal oppression. The lovers cannot get married while they are alive, but cannot give up their pursuit of each other after death. Readers found their dogged persistence and blazing love most moving. Examples are "Polishing the Jade Boddhisatva" (see *Popular Novels of the Capital*) and "The Emotional Zhou Shengxian Plays Havoc in the Fan Pavilion Restaurant" (see *Immortal Words for Awaking the World*, edited by Feng Menglong).

In the urban literature stories of love and marriage the images of women tend to be fully delineated, while those of men tend to be flat and colorless. The characters of the women are either fiery and unyielding or soft and gentle; either way they arouse our sympathy and admiration. The men, on the other hand, tend to be weaklings or snobs, and arouse our distaste. From the time of the Song Dynasty more and more bonds of feudal ethics were placed on women, and yet in the works of urban literature the images of women are bright and cheerful. This is an interesting phenomenon that merits deeper study.

Politics and history

The "storytelling" style of novel, which arose in the Southern Song Dynasty (1127–1279), can be divided into four categories. One is the historical novel. Guan Punai (Deweng) says in his "A Record of the Capital's Landscape": "Historical novels deal with the vicissitudes and wars of past dynasties, based on historical literary tradition."[5] As examples of this type of novel, we may cite the five stories in *The Five Kinds of Illustrated Vernacular Fictions*, which was published in the Zhizhi reign period (1321–1323) of the Yuan Dynasty, including *King Wu Marches against the Tyrant Zhouh*, *Annals of the Seven States*, *Qin Annexes Six Other States*, *History of the Former Han Dynasty* and *Annals of the Three*

Kingdoms in Plain Language. The latter provided the most important episodes of the later novel *Romance of the Three Kingdoms.* In addition, there was the *Anecdotes of the Great Song Dynasty*, out of which grew the *Outlaws of the Marsh.* The *Anecdotes* is an early depiction, if a somewhat simplified one, of the activities of the gang of outlaw heroes of Liangshan Marsh. *Romance of the Three Kingdoms* and *Outlaws of the Marsh* are the outstanding representatives of this genre.

Politics and history are major themes of Yuan Dynasty dramatic works too. The plot of "Guan Yu Meets His Formidable Foe with His Long Sword Alone" by Guan Hanqing is taken from the history of the Three Kingdoms period; that of *Rain on the Parasol Tree* by Bai Pu is based on the story of the liaison between Emperor Xuanzong of the Tang Dynasty and his concubine Lady Yang; that of *Autumn in the Han Palace* by Ma Zhiyuan is based on the historical tale of Master Wang Zhao going beyond the Great Wall; that of "Zhao the Orphan" by Ji Junxiang is based on a story of a feud between the two families of Tu and Zhao in the time of King Jing and Duke Ling of Jin during the Warring States Period. In addition, *Longevity Hall* by Hong Sheng and *The Peach Blossom Fan* by Kong Shangren, both of the early Qing Dynasty, belong here as they aim to sum up the lessons of history.

The historical and political content of urban literature, as it appears in dramas and novels, in fact served the function of primers of historical and political enlightenment, and had a deep and lasting social influence.

Knight-errant and courtroom fiction

In the four types of "storytelling literature" we find "Where complicated legal cases are concerned, they almost all involve the use of swords and sticks as well as the vicissitudes of fate and luck."[6] Clearly both knight-errant and courtroom fiction are combined in these works. Viewed from the angle of the actual conditions of urban literature, usually the work can be considered one or the other; but so as not to chop up the categories too finely, according to "A Record of the Capital's Landscape," we can discuss "storytelling literature" as a work which comprises both these themes.

A fairly early courtroom novel was "The Wrongfully Executed Cui Ning" (see *Popular Novels of the Capital*), which appears in the Song and Yuan prompt books. And a similarly early knight-errant novel is "Mr. Song Number Four Causes Trouble for Miser Zhang" (see *Novels Ancient and Modern.*). A large number of courtroom novels were produced in the later part of the Ming Dynasty. Their themes were no longer the gloomy ones of oppression by cruel officials, but turned to praising the incorruptibility of upright officials and their impartial investigations. An example can be found in *The Story of Mr. Hai Gangfeng Sitting in Judgment* (also called *The Story of Judge Hai*), edited by Li Chunfang. This novel tells of the judgments of Hai Rui, the magistrate of Chun'an County during the Ming Dynasty. *The Case of the Picture of the Dragon* (author unknown) is the story of an upright scholar of the Picture of the Dragon Bureau and how Bao Zheng, magistrate of Kaifeng, solves his case. In the Qing Dynasty courtroom and knight-errant themes were combined. For instance, *Magistrate Shi's Case* (author unknown) has greenwood outlaws mixed up with a court case decided by Shi Shilun, magistrate of Jiangdu County during the Kangxi reign period of the Qing Dynasty. Modern novels such as *Junior Heroes* by Wen Kangzhuan and *Three Gallants and Five Chivalrous Deeds* also belong here. The latter novel, in 120 chapters, was published in 1879, the fifth year of the reign of Qing Emperor Guangxu, and was assembled on the basis of *Judge Bao's Cases*, an opera script written by storytelling artist Shi Yukun. Later, it was improved upon by Yu Yue, and became very popular as *Seven Gallants and Five Chivalrous Deeds*. In this novel, Judge Bao Zheng is assisted by greenwood outlaws to investigate cases and right injustices. Included are also stories of intrigues between the outlaws themselves.

Among courtroom dramas should be mentioned Guan Hanqing's *The Injustice Done to Dou E* and *The Rice Seller of Chenzhou* by an anonymous person. The former draws on the story of the "filial daughter of Donghai" from the *History of the Han Dynasty*, but its main plot is based on the social conditions of the Yuan Dynasty, when Guan Hanqing lived. Through the false imprisonment of Dou E, the play reveals the dark side of that society and the political corruption that flourished then. It also, through the image of Dou E, lauds the fighting spirit of the people who opposed the oppressive government. *The Rice Seller of Chenzhou* tells how Judge Bao Zheng goes to Chengzhou to right an injustice. This play starkly reveals the wicked deeds of the corrupt officials, both high and low, of the Yuan Dynasty. The wit and humor of Judge Bao give a comedic color to this drama, and highlight its serious message.

The main purport of this type of literary works is to praise and extol upright officials. And the common characteristics of this type of literary works are the anguish of the common people suffering all kinds of social evils, and the hopes that they place in the honest officials that they will right the wrongs done to them. There is a clear distinction made between right and wrong, and the emotional coloring of these works is a strong one.

Tales of the supernatural

Among the storytelling works of the Song Dynasty was a special subgenre called "shuojing," that is, the recitation of Buddhist tales, which evolved from the form of explanation in verse and prose of the Buddhist precepts during the Tang Dynasty. *The Journey for the Buddhist Scriptures of Xuanzang of the Great Tang*, which was published in the Southern Song and Yuan Dynasties, contains a selection of such stories in storytellers' prompt-book form. The poetic drama *Xuanzang of Tang's Journey to the West in Search of the Buddhist Scriptures* by Wu Changling of the Yuan Dynasty contains a few of the lyric verses from that book. In the early part of the Ming Dynasty appeared the *Journey to the West in Verse-and-Prose Style*. It is cited in the Yong Le Encyclopedia, Volume 13139 in the categories of the rhymes "song" (send) and "meng" (dream). Previous to this, a version of this story is found in a Chinese-language textbook produced in Korea, titled, *Translated Version of Park's Translation. Journey to the West*, written by Wu Cheng'en of the middle part of the Ming Dynasty, is a full-length novel of the supernatural based on versions of the story which circulated in previous eras. Another full-length supernatural novel of the Ming Dynasty is *Enshrined as Spirits*, edited by Xu Zhonglin, who went by the sobriquet of "The Old Recluse of Bell Mountain." It tells of King Wu of Zhou's expedition to overthrow the tyrant Zhouh, last king of the Shang Dynasty (16th century – 11th century BC). Its plot mingles the spirit world with Buddhism. The Chan doctrine helps King Wu, and the Jie doctrine comes to the aid of King Zhouh. The former represents orthodox Taoism, and is in league with Buddhism, all the time helping King Wu and Jiang Ziya to promote the Confucian doctrine of righteous government. On this basis, the three religions coalesce. Finally the kings of Shang and Zhou, and their generals have their names inscribed on the list of supernatural beings. Other novels of the Ming Dynasty with supernatural themes are *Supplement to the Journey to the West* by Dong Shuo, *An Account of Sansui Defeating the Evil Spirits* by Luo Guanzhong (20 chapters) and Feng Menglong (40 chapters), and *The Story of Zhong Kui* (Liu Zhang of the early Qing period considered this to be the basis for the 10th chapter of the fourth volume of *The Story of the Ghost Slayer*).

Cautionary and didactic

An important part of urban literature is works which describe the ways of the world and offer cautionary instruction. The so-called "ways of the world" covers a broad scope: The portrayal of all kinds of behavior, including the fickleness of people; the fetters of fame and wealth; sudden "rags to riches" transformations; displays of ingratitude and hankering after pleasure while turning the back on righteous conduct are all grist to the mill of urban literature. At the same time, most of these works contained an element of warning or satire. Some catered directly to the tastes of the urban readers or listeners, and often highlight low and vulgar matters. The cautionary content of such works is slight. This type of writing is somewhat similar in tone to the *fu* poems of the Han Dynasty – "admonish one hundred but satirize only one." It comes from an ancient tradition. Ancient Chinese literature always had a strongly didactic function, and this orthodox viewpoint exerted an unavoidable influence on urban literature too. So there is always a strain of instruction in the entertainment. However, the instruction and admonition of urban literature are always along the lines of the ideology of the feudal ruling class and its Three Cardinal Guides (ruler guides subject, father guides son and husband guides wife) and Five Constant Virtues (benevolence, righteousness, propriety, wisdom and fidelity), and this can frequently be glimpsed. Nevertheless, a call to resist the feudal ethics can be heard from time to time. It could be said that the cautionary and didactic form of urban literature is the most complicated and interesting of that genre.

As early as in the Song and Yuan Dynasties we find a number of elements of cautionary and didactic tales in the literature. "The Upright Supervisor Zhang" tells how the owner of a business, a man in his 60s named Zhang Shilian, marries a young girl. The latter falls in love with Zhang Sheng, the young supervisor of the shop, but he spurns her advances. Even after her death, she appears to Zhang Sheng, offering him a heap of jewels if he will marry her. But young Zhang still refuses, and because of this avoids misfortune. The story ends with, "Even facing death, Zhang Sheng kept himself pure and upright. Right to the end he remained unsullied, rising above worldly concerns. These days not one person in 10,000 is as free from avarice and lust as Zhang Sheng. There is a poem which praises him thus: 'Who is not given over to greed and lechery?/But from beginning to end it is difficult to corrupt a pure-hearted person/If a young man follows Zhang Sheng's example/He will have nothing to fear from either ghosts or men.'"[7] Likewise, "Concubine Qiao Yanjie Breaks Up a Family" from *Ordinary Words to Alarm the World* and "Fifteen Jokes that Miscarried" from *Immortal Words for Awaking the World* belong to this genre. The "Three Words" of the book of that title – admonishing the world, startling the world and awakening the world – all have a cautionary meaning.

Pride of place among the cautionary and admonitory full-length novels of the Ming and Qing Dynasties is held by the *Plum in a Golden Vase*. Composed of 100 chapters, this novel paints a broad picture of daily urban life in China in the 16th century. In the process, it describes the dark and corrupt society of the late Ming Dynasty through the events in the life of the official, rich merchant and local tyrant Ximen Qing and his family. The author's aim was to warn his contemporaries by presenting Ximen Qing as a model of how not to behave. Xin Xinzi, in his "Preface to the *Ci* Rendition of Plum in a Golden Vase," says, "The language is fresh, and the novel enjoys wide popularity. It enlightens people as to morality, and warns them against lechery. It points out the difference between chaste and unchaste behavior, and between good and evil in general. The wheel of fortune revolves before our eyes, and virtue and vice get their just desserts." In his "Commentary on the Novel *Plum in a Golden Vase*," Dong Wunong (Zhuke) says, "It is a warning to the world, not an encouragement."[8] It seems that this was indeed the author's main intention, but his work contains an element of satire, and he does not fully and objectively achieve his aim." *The Scholars*, by Wu Jingzi of the Qing Dynasty, is described by Lu Xun in his *A Brief History of the Chinese Novel* as a "satirical novel." As such, it can be ranked among the "novels of censure of the closing years of the Qing Dynasty," such as *Notes on the Present State of Officialdom* by Li Baojia, *Strange Situations Observed over Twenty Years* by Wu Woyao and *The Travels of Lao Can* by Liu E. All these works belong in the "cautionary and admonitory" category. In his *A Brief History of the Chinese Novel*, Lu Xun discusses *Plum in a Golden Vase* as a "cautionary novel of the Ming Dynasty," and *A Dream of Red Mansions* as a similar work of the Qing Dynasty. The latter work too belongs in the "cautionary and admonitory" category.

The protagonists of *The Scholars* are intellectuals, and it is through them that the novel satirizes the civil service system of traditional China. A lot of them are described as despicable types, such as Confucian scholars eager for fame, others who are steeped in the stereotyped "eight-legged essay," others whose only motive for study is greed for official rank, and others who browbeat and swindle their way around. The rottenness and heartlessness of this society come alive under the writing brush of author Wu Jingzi.

Cao Xueqin includes a wide variety of topics in his *A Dream of Red Mansions*, ranging from love and marriage, politics and history, and the snobbish ways of the world to the fickleness of fortune. The author betrays some elementary democratic thinking inasmuch as he makes scathing criticisms of every aspect of the society of his time and its various institutions, not to mention the ideology of the feudal ruling group, and even puts forward some vaguely democratic ideas and suggestions. From the viewpoint of its description of the "ways of the world," this novel does a deep and thorough job. From the aspect of admonition, opinions differ about *A Dream of Red Mansions*. Nevertheless, it is a deep novel in this respect too. A late-Qing critic said,

> The book, written with great talent and insight, is filled with poetry, calligraphy, zither and chess playing, ornamented rhythmic prose, instrument-accompanied storytelling, handicraft, correspondence, lantern riddle guessing, couplet writing, horizontal boards inscribing, drinkers' wager game playing, and legal documentation, doctors, soothsayers, monks sitting in meditation and fortune tellers – they are all there, and anything contained in the books of tales and anecdotes can be found in *A Dream of Red Mansions*. Its plot is acted out from the imperial court above to farm fields and dilapidated temples below. Its personages include the highest ranks of the aristocracy, including imperial concubines and eunuchs, civil and military officials, titled ladies and princes, daughters of wealthy families and village crones, Confucian scholars and doctors, hangers-on of influential men and common farmers, craftsmen and traders, servants, petty officials, Buddhist and Taoist monks and nuns, female abbots, and performing artists, drunkards and rascals, thieves and cripples – not a single type is missed, and they are all described in a true-to-life way. Moreover, loyalty, filial piety and the chastity of widows are described, as are robbery and lechery, and all kinds of violent deaths, such as committing suicide by throwing oneself into a well or hanging oneself or swallowing gold or some other poison, or dashing one's brains out. There is also the accidental swallowing of gold pills and deadly scuffles. It is all there; every aspect of life is described. The author's talent is as all-encompassing as the ocean. As an encyclopedia of life, its value is inextinguishable.[9]

Notes

1 *New Ci Version of Plum in a Golden Vase*, woodblock print during the Wanli Period of the Ming Dynasty

2 *Collected Poems of the Music Bureau* by Guo Maoqian [Song Dynasty], Vol. 47, Zhonghua Book Company, 1979, Pp. 640, 689

3 *Brilliant Record of the Dream of the Eastern Capital*, Meng Yuanlao [Song Dynasty], Vol. 5, Shanghai Ancient Books Publishing House, 1979

4 *Records of the Chats of a Drunken Old Man*, Vol. 1 of the first collection, Classical Literature Publishing House, 1957, P. 3

5 *Series of Anecdotes of Martial Heroes*, Vol. 1, Jiangsu Guangling Ancient Woodblock Press, 1985

6 *Series of Anecdotes of Martial Heroes*, Vol. 1, Jiangsu Guangling Ancient Woodblock Press, 1985

7 *Popular Novels of the Capital*, Vol.13, Classical Literature Publishing House, 1954, P. 55

8 *New Ci Version of Plum in a Golden Vase*, woodblock print during the Wanli Period of the Ming Dynasty

9 *Candid Tales of a Stone* by Buddhist Jie Cang [Qing Dynasty]. See Yisu ed. *Compilation of Study Materials on Classical Literature * Dream of the Red Chamber Volume*, First Section, Zhonghua Book Company, 1963, P. 193

12 Rural literature

China has traditionally been an agricultural society. The vast majority of the country's settlements have been villages, and the overwhelming majority of the population have been farmers and agricultural laborers. The villages of this vast soil very early in history produced a splendid literature – the "Airs of the States" and the "Minor Court Hymns" sections from the *Book of Odes*, a collection of poems and ballads compiled between the 11th and sixth centuries BC. Among these compilations are songs of protest at exploitation and oppression, and poems which reflect the lives of conscript laborers and problems of love and marriage, and ordinary working life. "A hungry man sings about food, while a laboring man sings of his work": This is the type of earthy flavor that pervades these songs and ballads. The "Airs of Bin * Seventh Month" has 88 lines of verse in eight sections. It describes the feelings of the farmers concerning their life and work in the order of the seasons. "Cutting Down a Hardwood Tree" and "Large Rat" from the "Airs of Wei" section of the *Book of Odes* accuse the slave-owners of doing no work while enjoying the fruits of others' labor, and at the same time show a yearning for a happy life. The "Airs of Bin * Eastern Mountain" expresses the tangled feelings of a man conscripted to serve in the army. "Airs of Zheng * The Rivers of Qin and Wei" has as its theme the custom of a youth and maiden going on a spring outing in the third month. "Zhounan * Hanguang" is a song sung by a woodcutter who is head-over-heels in love:

> In the south rise the trees without branches,
> Affording no shelter.
> By the Han girls are rambling about.
> But it is vain to solicit them.
> The breadth of the Han cannot be dived across.
> The length of the Jiang
> Cannot be navigated with a raft.
> Many are the bundles of firewood;
> I would cut down the thorns [to form more].
> Those girls that are going to their future home,
> I would feed their horses.

The breadth of the Han
Cannot be dived across;
The length of the Jiang,
Cannot be navigated with a raft.
Many are the bundles of firewood;
I would cut down the southern wood [to form more].
Those girls that are going to their future home,
I would feed their colts.
The breadth of the Han
Cannot be dived across;
The length of the Jiang
Cannot be navigated with a raft.[1]

The Han Dynasty's Music Bureau also collected some folk songs which had their roots in the rural villages, for instance, the "South of the River," which is put to a tune used to accompany a folk dance depicting lotus picking, and "At Fifteen I Followed the Army's March," which describes a conscript soldier's return home, where he finds no kin left to grieve for him.

After the Tang Dynasty there are few materials with respect to rural literature, but the few that remain still betray the special features of this genre. For instance, the "Nursery Rhymes of the Yongchun Emperor's Mid-reign" from *A New History of the Tang Dynasty * The Five Elements*:

The new millet does not go in the basket,
The new maize does not go to the threshing floor.
When the eighth or ninth month comes around,
Dogs bark behind the empty garden's wall.[2]

During the peasant uprisings that market the closing years of the Tang and Yuan Dynasties, ballads with a rural flavor spread widely across the country. For instance, *Ancient and Modern Anecdotes Written at Leisure*, which is the title of the 45th volume in the series *A Record of Yuan Poetry*, contains the following:

Heaven is high and the emperor is far away,
There are too few working people and too many dandies.
When one is beaten three times a day, what can one do but revolt?[3]

"Poem of Distress," from Volume 27 of the *Halt to Plowing*, contains the following:

Heaven sends a demon army,
To extirpate injustice.
The unjust kill the unjust.
When all injustice is wiped out,
Then will come a period of Great Peace.

The "Fuchun River Rhymes" in the *Zhi (Wisdom)* chapter of *Miscellaneous Records of the Jujube Forest* contains the words, "The fish were fat when I sold my son/The fragrant tea ruined my family," and the following curse: "Fuyang Mountain, when will you tumble down?/Fuyang River, when will you dry up?"[4] A children's song from the end of the Ming Dynasty goes like this:

> He eats off his wife,
> He is clothed by his wife.
> He has opened the main gate to welcome King Chuang,
> When King Chuang comes, he doesn't pay his tax grain.[5]

Li Yan (originally Li Xin), who later joined Li Zicheng's rebellion, wrote the poem "The Song of Persuasion for Disaster Relief":

> Plagues of locusts happen frequently by the year-end,
> Destroying crops they make the harvest impossible.
> As the price of rice is soaring now,
> People are living on the edge of starvation everywhere.
> Grass roots and tree leaves are eaten to satisfy hunger;
> Going without food, young children cry face to face.
> The rice pots are so dry that they've gathered a lot of dust,
> A meal of soup may hardly be available many days.
> Grain levy collectors act like preying tigers;
> Rich families collect land rent with the hearts of wolves.
> Poor farmers are left lingering on with their last breath,
> Their souls already struggling in the underworld.
> Skeletons of the starved are piled high in mounds,
> Even the moneyed find it hard to stave off hunger.
> How can this stark situation not make us cry?
> We can find blood spots in the tears we're shedding.
> I urge you rich families to be liberal with your relief;
> Grain from your granary is a boundless blessing.
> To bring back to life a person of skin and bone,
> Requires nothing more than a change of heart.
> Selfless Heaven always blesses the kind-hearted;
> Benevolence helps one accumulate virtue and happiness.
> Helping the poor and the needy is a great deed,
> And accumulated virtues will enrich your posterity.[6]

Li Yan was a native of Qi County in Henan Province, the son of an official of the Military Affairs Bureau. He was originally a landowner, but he opened his granaries to feed starving people, and also wrote poems encouraging others to do the same. His philanthropy made him enemies among the well-to-do, and he was eventually arrested and thrown into prison. This enraged the ordinary people of the county, who rescued him, killing the county magistrate in the process. Li Yan then joined the rebel forces of Li Zicheng.

The following ballad is a heartfelt cry of the rural people which swept through the countryside at the time of the peasant uprisings at the end of the Ming Dynasty. It is contained in the 11th section of the *Leisurely Chat in a Bean Shack:* "Grandpa Heaven, you are advanced in years. Your hearing and sight are dim. You don't see the people, you don't hear their cries. Murderers and arsonists run rampant. Saints and scholars are starving to death. Grandpa Heaven, you are no longer fit to rule in Heaven. You have failed in your duty. Grandpa Heaven, you are no longer fit to rule in Heaven. You have failed in your duty."[7]

Rural folk songs saw another wave of popularity during the rebellion of the Taiping Heavenly Kingdom (1851–1864) during the Qing Dynasty. Some of them have passed down to the present day; farmers in the Changshu area south of the city of Suzhou in Jiangxi Province can still sing the folk song "Cherishing the Memory of the Taiping Army." Many local peasants in Changshu joined the Taipings, and when the latter were defeated the famers' wives made up this song: "The peas are all in flower, and their buds are red. My elder brother joined the Taiping army, but is now gone without a trace. I made some new farm clothes for him to wear, and built a new house for him to use. Now I see the wild geese flying south, but I never see my brother coming home."[8]

Popular legends are an important part of rural literature. The famous legend of the cowherd and the weaving maid, in which the man is a farmer and the girl is a weaver of cloth, reflects the small-scale peasant economy. As early as the time of the *Book of Odes*, in its "Minor Airs" section, the poem *Da Dong* is about weaving maids:

And the three stars together are the Weaving Sisters,
Passing in a day the seven stages of the sky.
Although they go through their seven stages,
Brilliantly shine the Draught Oxen.
But they do not serve to draw our carts.

Likewise, in the *Records of the Years of Jing Chu* by Zong Lin of the Liang Dynasty (502–557, one of the Southern Dynasties) we find reference to the story of the meeting of the Cowherd and the Weaving Maid: "The evening of the seventh day of the seventh (lunar) month is when the Cowherd and the Weaving Maid meet. In the evening, women make five-colored threads, leading them into the eyes of needles of gold, silver or stone. They also spread tables with wine, fruit and melons in the courtyard to pray for good needlework skills as a way of celebrating the legendary celestial lovers. The sight of a long-jawed spider weaving a web on the gourd vines in the yard was regarded as an auspicious sign that their prayers or wishes were answered."[9]

The second volume of the *Celestial Record* by Chen Yaowen of the Ming Dynasty has a storytelling flavor in this vein: "Legend has it that to the east of the

Milky Way was the Weaving Maid, the daughter of the Lord of Heaven. Year after year she plied her shuttle, weaving the brocade clouds, Heaven's raiment. The Lord of Heaven, feeling sorry that such a pretty girl should be alone, with no time for anything but work, married her to the Cowherd, who dwelt to the west of the Milky Way. However, following her marriage, the Weaving Maid began to neglect her work. This angered her father, who ordered the Weaving Maid to return to her old place east of the Milky Way, allowing the pair to meet only once a year."[10] The story of the Cowherd and the Weaving Maid is a widely known folk tale. There are many variations on the plot, but it is a classic example of rural literature.

Another example is the story of "The Old Man Who Moved the Mountains," which appeared in the *Tang Wen* chapter of the *Liezi*. The earliest version of this legend is in the *Spring and Autumn Pivot which Moves the Dipper*. It is also recorded in the *Biography of Ruan Xiaoxu* in the *History of the Liang Dynasty*, which is basically a legend about ginseng.[11] This story is still widely known today.

Just as China has a vast countryside, so it has a rich rural literature. As a result of painstaking investigations and re-arrangements by scholars from among the common people a large number of valuable works of this nature were produced, well worth delving deeply into. It is appropriate, therefore, to pay great attention to rural literature as a major genre of Chinese literature as a whole.

This section has divided Chinese literature into four general parts for discussion. By doing so, it has only been possible to give a simplified and overall view of the subject. Literary phenomena are complicated, and the subject of a literary work is often not simple. Without dividing the discussion up it is impossible to identify the key link, and so each division cannot help but tend toward simplification. When factors seem to be evenly balanced, identification of the key link becomes even more important, just as it is essential to grasp the main thread of a tangled skein. Moreover, I believe that these categories basically conform to reality. And it is only by stating outright that there is a complex facet to each category that one avoids over-simplification.

Notes

1 *Commentary on the Thirteen Classics*, World Bookstore photocopy of the Ruan woodblock print, PP. 281–282
2 Ouyang Xiu and Song Qi [Song Dynasty]: *A New History of the Tang Dynasty*, Vol. 25, *Section on the Five Elements*, Zhonghua Book Company, 1965, P. 919
3 Chen Yan [Qing Dynasty]: *A Record of Yuan Poetry*, The Commercial Press, 1936, P. 750
4 *Overview of Sketches and Novels*, Vol. 32, Jiangsu Guangling Ancient Woodblock Press, 1983
5 *The North Part of the Anecdotes of the Ming Dynasty*, Vol. 23, Zhonghua Book Company, 1984, P. 656
6 *The North Part of the Anecdotes of the Ming Dynasty*, Vol. 23, Zhonghua Book Company, 1984, P. 652
7 The Buddhist Ai Na ed. [Qing Dynasty]: *Leisurely Chat in a Bean Shack*, Shanghai Ancient Books Publishing House, 1983, P. 125
8 Yuan Fei ed.: *Miscellaneous Collection of Jiangsu Folk Songs*, Shanghai Culture Publishing House, 1955, P. 76

9 Zong Lin [Liang Dynasty, Southern Dynasties]: Records of the Years of Jing Chu, *Collected Literary Works*, first edition

10 Chen Yaowen [Ming Dynasty]: Celestial Record, Vol. 2, Wen Yuan Ge Publishing House, *Collected Writings of the Four Basic Branches of Literature*

11 The fifth volume of the *History of the Liang Dynasty*, titled, *Biography of Ruan Xiaoxu*, contains the following anecdote: "Ruan Xiaoxu's mother fell ill, and needed some ginseng, which was said to grow on Mount Bell, to take as medicine. Ruan Xiaoxu went personally into the wilds to search for some. For several days he had no luck, and then he suddenly saw a deer. Ruan Xiaoxu was strangely moved by the sight of the deer, and followed it. When it reached a certain place, the deer vanished. But, lo and behold! There on the ground was the ginseng the boy had been looking for. He took it home to his mother, and after taking it she made a full recovery." Zhonghua Book Company, 1973, P. 740

Part V

The allure of Chinese literature

The presence of Confucianism, Buddhism and Taoism in Chinese literature

The influence of the three schools of thought – Confucianism, Buddhism and Taoism – on Chinese literature can be discussed in two ways: One approach is from the view of the cosmos of each of the three and the way their views of man and ethical systems had an effect on the thought and creativity of writers. This is a complicated subject and involves an exposition of Chinese philosophical concepts, and therefore is outside the scope of this book. What this book will deal with, however, is the second aspect of this topic – the extent to which the three schools of thought permeated Chinese literature. But even so, I will confine myself to the following three outstanding questions: the connection between the poetic doctrine of the Confucianists and Chinese literature; the connection between Chan Buddhism and Chinese literature; and the connection between the naturalism of the Taoist masters Laozi and Zhuangzi and Chinese literature.

13 Confucian poetic doctrine and Chinese literature

Examples of the phrase "poetic doctrine" first appear in the *Book of Rites * Different Teaching of the Different Kings*:

> Confucius said, "When you enter any state you can know what subjects (its people) have been taught. If they show themselves men who are mild and gentle, sincere and good, they have been taught from the *Book of Odes*. If they have a wide comprehension and know what is remote and old, they have been taught from the *Book of Documents*. If they be large-hearted and generous, bland and honest, they have been taught from the *Book of Music*. If they be pure and still, refined and subtle, they have been taught from the *Book of Changes*. If they be courteous and modest, grave and respectful, they have been taught from the *Book of Rites*. If they suitably adapt their language to the things of which they speak, they have been taught from the *Spring and Autumn Annals*. Hence the failing that may arise in connection with the study of the *Book of Odes* is a stupid simplicity; that in connection with the *Book of Documents* is duplicity; that in connection with the *Book of Music* is extravagance; that in connection with the *Book of Changes* is the violation (of reason); that in connection with the *Book of Rites* is fussiness; and that in connection with the *Spring and Autumn Annals* is insubordination. If they show themselves men who are mild and gentle, sincere and good, and yet free from that simple stupidity, their comprehension of the *Book of Odes* is deep. If they have a wide comprehension of things and know what is remote and old, and yet are free from duplicity, their understanding of the *Book of Documents* is deep. If they are large-hearted and generous, bland and honest, and yet have no tendency to extravagance, their knowledge of the *Book of Music* is deep. If they are pure and still, refined and subtle, and yet do not violate reason they have made great attainments in the study of the *Book of Changes*. If they are courteous and modest, grave and reverent, and yet not fussy, their acquaintance with the *Book of Rites* is deep. If they suitably adapt their language to the things of which they speak, and yet have no disposition to be insubordinate, their knowledge of the *Spring and Autumn Annals* is deep."[1]

Poetic doctrine was the principal means of teaching the Six Arts – the Rites, Music, Archery, Charioteering, Writing and Mathematics. The classics dealing separately with these subjects were regarded by the people of the Han Dynasty as the Confucian scriptures. The *Book of Rites* was probably compiled by Confucianists of the Han Dynasty, and it is unlikely that the above quotation is in the words of Confucius himself; nevertheless, it reflects the genuine outlook of the Confucian school, and it had a very great influence on Chinese literature.

What does the quotation mean by "mild and gentle, sincere and good"? Kong Yingda, in his "Righteousness," an interpretation of the *Different Teaching of the Different Kings*, says, "Mild means a kindly face, and gentle means a nature of equanimity. The *Book of Odes* is ambivalent in its wording and avoids going straight to the heart of a matter, and so it can be said that it teaches one to be 'mild and gentle, sincere and good.'" Again, he says, "The *Book of Odes* stresses honesty and sincerity, but if one overdoes this, one can fall into a state of foolishness."[2] In ancient times there was a tradition of offering remonstrances to one's superiors couched in verse. In the *Conversations of the States * Conversations of Zhou, Part 1*," Duke Shao admonishes King Li as follows: "When Your Highness wishes to be advised as to government, you get your ministers to submit their proposals in verse form, and then you consider them. Kindly allow your humble servant to express his view that this is not a sensible procedure."[3] It can be seen that "mild and gentle, sincere and good" was meant as an attitude to be adopted when offering advice to a superior. Confucius says in the *Analects * Yang Huo*: "The *Odes* serve to stimulate the mind. They may be used for purposes of self-contemplation. They teach the art of sociability. They show how to regulate feelings of resentment." According to the commentary of Kong Anguo, "resentment" here means "a complaint directed at the government." When a poet expressed a complained about some deficiency in government, he had to keep his criticism within bounds and adopt an appropriate attitude, and this restriction and attitude had to be "mild and gentle, sincere and good" and keep within the bounds of propriety. The Confucianists' demand of poets was that they should be "mild and gentle, sincere and good," but not to the extent of becoming "foolish." Clearly, this literary viewpoint is an expression of Confucius' "Golden Mean" in the sphere of literature.

These four words "mild and gentle, sincere and good" have had a profound influence on Chinese literature. They have been both a standard to be abided by in the creative work of writers and a guideline for literary critics. However, the standard postulated by "mild and gentle, sincere and good" is hard to grasp, and when it comes to concrete works different people have different ideas. Wang Liu'an, of the Huainan school, says in his "Discussion of 'Li Sao'": "The 'Airs of the States' is romantic without being lascivious, the 'Minor Court Hymns' expresses censure without being insubordinate [both are sections of the *Book of Odes*]. 'Li Sao' can be said to embrace both these qualities."[4] In Wang Liu'an's opinion, the "Li Sao" is truly "mild and sincere, gentle and good." But Ban Gu, in his "Preface to 'Li Sao'" says, "That fellow Qu Yuan flaunted his talent and put on airs. He was always trying to alarm the people of his Kingdom of Chu. He made wild accusations of wrongdoing, even going so far as to censure the king and thereby arousing the enmity of Prime Minister Jiao Lan. In the end, unable to endure his sufferings and melancholy, he drowned himself in a river. All in all, he seems to have been a censorious and madcap fellow."[5] So he does not seem to think that Qu Yuan was sufficiently "mild and gentle, sincere and good." In his "Preface to the Syntactic and Semantic Analysis of Chu Poetry," Wang Yi writes, "The authors of the *Classic of Poetry* who satirized monarchs tended to say, 'Don't you know good from bad? . . . Although I'm not addressing you in person, my words sound as if I were talking into your ear." The satirical language found in the poems of the *Book of Odes* is particularly severe. However, in his commentary, Confucius still classified them as belonging to the "Major Court Hymns." In comparison, is Qu Yuan's language, though seemingly moderate, not akin to grabbing a monarch's ear to criticize his folly? Nevertheless, Ban Gu and his like thought that by satirizing the monarch and blaming him against his will, the satirists were showing off their talent to promote themselves. By saying so, Ban and his people are really being unfair.[6] The author criticizes Ban Gu's judgment of Qu Yuan, giving it as his opinion that Qu Yuan's carefree and gentle nature was in accord with the norm of being "mild and gentle, sincere and good." The Tang Dynasty poet Bai Juyi's "Songs of Qinzhong" and "New Yuefu Poems" raise the question of whether he is in accord with the norm of being "mild and gentle, sincere and good." In his "A Letter to Yuan Zhen," Bai Juyi says,

> On listening to my "Songs of Qinzhong," the wealthy, the influential, and the monarch's intimate ministers all turn pale and gaze at each other in speechless despair. On listening to "A Pleasant Visit to a Garden" that I wrote to you, those in power all feel flabbergasted. On listening to my "Staying at Purple Pavilion Village," those who control military power all clench their teeth in hatred. Things have happened roughly like that, but I cannot list them one by one. Those who do not want to befriend me dismiss me either as fishing for fame or as slandering. Those who are on good terms with me exhort me by using Niu Zengru as an example, as he was exiled for his frank criticism of current politics. Even my close relatives, including my wife and children, think that I am in the wrong. Those who think of me as being correct are but two or three in the entire world.[7]

What Bai Juyi advocates in his poems shares the same line of descent as the Confucian discussions, and so he regards his poems as in line with the tradition of poetic doctrine. Others, however, disagree, accusing him of "slander" and "ridicule." The jury is still out deliberating this matter.

Nevertheless, the fact that the "mild and gentle, sincere and good" poetic doctrine may allow some presupposition of subtle advice or complaint to a sovereign throws a lifeline for the continuance of this type of Chinese literature inasmuch as the writer can express his feelings toward government and reality as a whole – even to the extent of criticism or complaint – without withdrawing completely from government or avoiding the thorny problems of real life. It was precisely this type of vigorous literary creation that produced Du Fu and Bai Juyi. At the same time, because of the four bonds of "mild and gentle, sincere and good," writers had to use diplomatic language and indirect references, and this gave Chinese literature one kind of traditional attraction. When a writer used his brush to try to mend deficiencies in government and the life around him, he had to stick to the road of moderation, which was a difficult thing to do.

To illustrate "mild and gentle, sincere and good," I would like to cite a work by the late-Tang poet She Yi, "In Praise of Farm Life":

> I sold my new silk before nurturing my silkworms,
> I sold my new grain just after planting my seedlings.
> It's like binding a wound that hurts for now,
> By cutting out a piece of flesh from my heart.
> Deeply I am cherishing a wish for the monarch,
> That his heart may light up like a candle flame,
> Shining not only on the table of his lavish food
> But also on the houses forsaken by the hopeless.[8]

The meaning of this poem is: The second month is already here, and the silk strands have not yet been gathered. The fifth month is already here, and the harvest has not yet been brought in. The farmers are expecting that the new silk and the new crops will have to be sold cheaply. Even if they can catch up with the busy work before them, they wonder how life can go on like this, always utilizing stop-gap measures. The poet says, "I wish the emperor's heart could become as bright as a glittering candle. That candle should not just shed its beams upon the houses of the titled and wealthy and sumptuous feasts, but on the hovels of the fugitives from poverty." He means that he hopes that the emperor will pay attention to the sufferings of the people. As the poet confronts the contrast between the poor and the rich, and the tribulations of the ordinary people, he is at a loss how to solve such problems, and can only entrust his hope to the emperor. This poem can be regarded as a model of the "mild and gentle, sincere and good."

Notes

1 *Commentary on the Thirteen Classics*, World Bookstore photocopy of the Ruan wood-block print, P. 1609
2 *Commentary on the Thirteen Classics*, World Bookstore photocopy of the Ruan wood-block print, P. 1609
3 *Conversations of the States * Conversations of Zhou, Part 1*, Shanghai Ancient Books Publishing House, 1978, P. 9
4 Sima Qian [Han Dynasty]: *Records of the Historian*, Vol.84, *Biography of Qu Yuan*, Zhonghua Book Company, 1982, P. 2481
5 Hong Xingzu [Song Dynasty]: *Additional Commentary on the Songs of Chu*, Vol. 1, Zhonghua Book Company, 1983, p. 49
6 Hong Xingzu [Song Dynasty]: *Additional Commentary on the Songs of Chu*, Vol. 1, Zhonghua Book Company, 1983, p. 49
7 Bai Juyi [Tang Dynasty]: *The Changqing Collection About a Woman With the Name Bai*, Vol. 45, Ancient Literature Publishing House, 1955
8 *Complete Tang Poems*, Vol. 636, Zhonghua Book Company, 1960, P. 7296

14 Chan Buddhism and Chinese literature

Chan is a transliteration of the Sanskrit word "Dhyana," which means meditation, a type of self-cultivation highly valued by all of India's Buddhist sects. But India never produced a proper Chan sect, which was a creation of Chinese Buddhism. Following its solid establishment during the Tang Dynasty, Chan had a broad influence on the literati, penetrating their everyday lives, patterns of thought and even their artistic tastes. At the same time, Chan formed an indissoluble bond with poetry, and later even with other genres of literature. The connection between Chan and the novel *A Dream of Red Mansions* is very clear indeed. However, to avoid overstepping the boundaries of the topic of this book, we will confine ourselves to discussing the very important connection that Chan has with Chinese poetry.

The infiltration of Chan into Chinese poetry can nowadays be viewed from two angles:

The first is the way Chan thought penetrated poetry, both directly and indirectly. Poems which directly adopted Chan terms and Chan principles have the outward form of poems but not the esthetic value of poetry. These we will leave for the time being. What are worth paying attention to are those poems in which Chan ideas "drip from the brush and the ink." These don't preach Chan doctrines directly, but the flavor of Chan comes across in their descriptions of scenery and everyday life. For instance, in the poems of Wang Wei we can find concentrated expressions of the three realms of evanescence, emptiness and quietude, which are the very pursuits of Chan. Wang Wei himself was in fact an admirer of Chan Buddhism, which tended to flavor his life and thoughts, and so when he wrote poems the influence of Chan naturally but subtly changed their whole atmosphere. Chan's doctrine insists on emptying one's mind of thought, and chooses emptiness as the essence of human existence, which means emptying the heart of all desire, all striving, all life and all death – until the realm of great rest and great quietude is reached. In some of his landscape poems, Wang Wei includes not a single Chan term; he borrows natural scenery to express his mind. Nevertheless, readers of his poems can feel the meaning of Chan in them. For instance, his poem "The Mulan Magnolia Basin": "On the tips of the branches the hibiscus flowers blossom. The mountains are red with blooms. The valley is hushed, not a soul is there. No one to see the riot of flowers awaken and die. In the solitary mountain gorge the hibiscus flowers blossom and fall/Just as there is no one to see them open and perish/So they know nothing of the changes of the world."[1] On this, Hu Yinglin commented, "The reader of this poem forgets both himself and the world. All his thoughts dissolve into quietude."[2] Another example is his "A Deer Park":

> In the empty mountains not a soul is seen,
> But suddenly I hear the sound of voices.
> I betake myself into the thicket deep,
> But even here a sunbeam drops upon the moss.[3]

Just as the far-off sound of human voices jars the silence of the mountain, so does a beam of sunlight obtrude into a thick forest and highlight a patch of green moss. The brilliant light of day, now fading, lingers into the dusk. The contrasts here all indicate change – of light, of warmth, of color tone. The highlighting of the green moss symbolizes the coming into being and the passing away of the myriad things of the world. Nothing is unchanging.

However, more important than the infiltration of Chan into poetry is the fact that Chan gives rise to discussion about poetic creativity and appreciation. Chan's stress on innermost experience and analogy, and its pursuit of the "meaning outside the words" have an inspirational effect on poetic creativity and appreciation. Every one of the three stanzas of *A Study of Poetry Versified* by Wu Ke of the later part of the Song Dynasty starts with "The study of poetry is very much like the study of Chan meditation."[4] The first stanza combines the "gradual cultivation of the northern school of Chan with the "sudden enlightenment" of the southern school to reveal the course of the learning of poetic creativity, i.e., a long time spent in cultivation leading to sudden realization – the reaching of a state of effortless mastery. The second stanza is against following in the footsteps of those who have gone before, and stresses personal enlightenment. Chan does not need elaborate scriptures, and is against accepting others' precepts uncritically or "stealing others' words," even going so far as to dare to mock the ancestors and berate Buddha himself. The main tenet of Chan is that each person's nature arises from that very person, and if that person can truly perceive that nature he or she can become a Buddha. From the Chan point of view, the composition of poetry is just the same. The third stanza regards the "achievement" aimed at by Chan as the highest realm of poetry.

Yan Yu set great store by the Chan outlook in poetry. In his *Canglang's Remarks on Poetry*, he contrasts "academic achievement" with "enlightenment," giving priority to the latter. "Enlightenment" is a special form of intelligent awakening or inspiration. It can express at the same time the insights of Chan and artistic feelings: "It is only through enlightenment that one reaches the way of Chan, and only through enlightenment that one reaches the way of poetry."[5] On the basis of enlightenment one should be willing to study; when studying, one should aspire to the ultimate. Only then can one hope to attain the sublimity of poetry. "Penetrating to the depths of exquisiteness does not involve merely appreciating concrete things. It is like sounds in the air, the beauty of a face, the moon in the water or the form in a mirror, because the words have a limit but the meaning is limitless."[6] This type of poetry, which gives the reader limitless enlightenment through limited words, has manifold interpretations, and it is just because of the latter that it does not stop at any particular interpretation. Moreover, it is just for the same reason that Chan cannot be completely grasped from any particular angle. That is why it is said to be like "sounds in the air, the beauty of a face, the moon in the water or the form in a mirror."

To sum up, the function of the personal enlightenment stressed in Chan-influenced poetry on the course of poetic creation and appreciation, and the apportioning of interest and reasoning, is to bestow on such poetry a high artistic standard in which limited words and unlimited meaning are combined in harmony. These are the aspects of Chinese literature that help us to understand its allure.

Notes

1 Zhao Diancheng [Qing Dynasty]: *Collected Works of Wang Youcheng With Notes and Comments*, Vol. 13, Shanghai Ancient Books Publishing House, 1984, P. 249
2 Hu Yinglin [Ming Dynasty]: *Garland of Poetry*, Privately collated, Vol. 6, Shanghai Ancient Books Publishing House, 1979, P. 119
3 Zhao Diancheng [Qing Dynasty]: *Collected Works of Wang Youcheng With Notes and Comments*, Vol. 13, Shanghai Ancient Books Publishing House, 1984, P. 243
4 Wu Ke, in his *A Study of Poetry Versified*, says, "The study of poetry is like Buddhist meditation/One does not count the years spent on the bamboo couch or prayer mat/ One continues until the goal is reached/Until all worldly things are transcended." And "Learning to write poems is as natural as meditating. Being affected and artificial is not recommendable. Leaving the track of our worthy predecessors, you will find your aspirations soaring into the sky." And "How often since ancient times has perfection been attained?/This cosmos-shaking feat until now?" *Exquisite Fragments From the Poets*, Vol. 1, Zhonghua Book Company Shanghai Editorial Office, 1961, P. 8
5 Guo Shaoyu (editor and interpreter): *Canglang's Remarks on Poetry * Discussing Poems*, Shanghai Ancient Books Publishing House, 1962, P. 10
6 *Canglang's Remarks on Poetry * Discussing Poems*, Shanghai Ancient Books Publishing House, 1962, P. 24

15 The naturalism of Laozi, Zhuangzi and Chinese literature

We first find the word "nature" in the book called *Laozi:* "Man takes his law from the Earth; the Earth takes its law from Heaven; Heaven takes its law from the Dao. The law of the Dao is its being what it is."[1] The word used here, "nature," is not what we call nature today, but the existence of a thing in its original appearance, its evolution in accordance with innate laws without any reliance on external conditions or forces. The book *Laozi* the word "nature" is often encountered. For instance, in the following: "Their work was done and their undertakings were successful, while the people all said, 'We are as we are, of ourselves!'" "Abstaining from speech marks him who is obeying the spontaneity of his nature," and "This honoring of the Dao and exalting of its operation is not the result of any ordination, but always a spontaneous tribute."[2] Here, the word "nature" means something like spontaneity or "it is of itself." According to the *Laozi*, there are four great entities in the universe – Man, Earth, Heaven and the Dao (the Way). Man takes his laws from Earth; Earth takes its laws from Heaven. Heaven takes its laws from the Dao, and the Dao is a law unto itself. There is no need for the Dao to take its laws from anything outside itself. The Dao is the highest and deepest of the four great entities. The existence of the Dao preceded that of all the myriad things on Earth and in Heaven. Before Laozi himself, people thought that Heaven was the father of everything. But Laozi investigated where Heaven itself came from, and concluded that the Dao came before Heaven, and was the root of Heaven. Before Laozi, people thought that the Lord of Heaven was the supreme ruler, and that all changes took place at the behest of the Lord of Heaven. Laozi, however, denied that Heaven had a will. He maintained that the myriad things sprang from the Dao, and that this gestation was spontaneous and occurred without any purpose. And so the Dao itself took no action, and yet did everything: "The Dao in its regular course does nothing (for the sake of doing it), and so there is nothing which it does not do."[3] Zhuangzi inherited the naturalism of Laozi, saying, "Rites are prescribed for the practice of the common people; man's proper Truth is what he has received from Heaven, operating spontaneously, and unchangeable. Therefore the sages take their law from Heaven, and prize their (proper) Truth, without submitting to the restrictions of custom. The stupid do the reverse of this. They are unable to take their law from Heaven, and are influenced by other men; they do not know how to prize the proper Truth (of their nature), but are under the dominion of ordinary things, and change according to the customs (around them): always, consequently, incomplete."[4] The two basic viewpoints of the naturalism of Laozi and Zhuangzi are "taking nature as the law" and "prizing truth."

The infiltration of the naturalism of Laozi and Zhuangzi into Chinese literature was mainly in the form of the pursuit of the establishment of "nature" in both literary creation and literary criticism.

The core thought of Tao Yuanming, a leading poet of the Eastern Jin Dynasty, was "returning to Nature." Nature was the supreme standard guiding his life and creativity. "Too long was I fenced in/Now I have returned to Nature /Embracing the simple and the true" (*Guiyuantianju*). Here, the "simple" and the "true" indicate a pure human nature, unspotted by ceremony or learning. The first is a nod at *Laozi*, the second a nod at *Zhuangzi*. Tao Yuanming was not the sort of man to demean himself for the sake of a fat salary. He returned to his farm and cultivated the land himself, supplying his own needs. Completely unperturbed, he put into practice the ideal of a natural life he so clung to. As a result, his poetic creations embodied a sort of beauty of nature. His poems are neither artificial nor ornate, but unaffected and natural, and succeed in bringing out the true and unsullied hues of nature. The subjects he writes about are often commonplace. There is seldom any special imagery or flowery language; nevertheless, the effect is strikingly beautiful. Tao Yuanming, in fact, occupies an exalted position in the history of Chinese literature by blazing a trail to reach the beauty of nature in the literary field by drawing on the naturalism of Laozi and Zhuangzi.

The influence of the thought of Laozi and Zhuangzi was also deep on the works of the great Tang poet Li Bai, as his poetic creation too sought a kind of natural beauty. But he and Tao Yuanming had different personalities, and their individual expressions of nature were very different. Nevertheless, the "Nature" they sought was the same. In his *A Poem to Wei Liangzai*, Li Bai says, "The lotus emerges from the clear water/Exquisitely decorated by Nature" (from "A Poem of Emotional Expression that I Give to Governor Wei Liangzai as I Recollect the Past Visit during My Exile in Yelang after My Release to Jiangxia by the Emperor's Kindness"). These two lines encapsulate the very poetic style Li Bai strove for. In the 35th poem of his *Ancient Style*, he excoriates "the ugly woman who assumed a frown" (in imitation of a famous beauty) and "man who copied the Handan walk" (in imitation of the supposed sophisticates of the city of Handan): "By showing off one's literary skill one is merely ornamenting a worm and losing the intrinsic beauty of Nature." He uses the words "natural" and "unaffected" to mean the same thing – the quintessential beauty of nature, which is what he pursues in his poetic creation. That Li Bai attained his sublime objective we can see when we read his "Sound of a Flute on a Spring Night in Luoyang":

> The spring breeze carries with it,
> The notes of a jade flute.
> From somewhere they are wafted,
> Through the whole of Luoyang City.
> Among the airs this night,

Is the tune "Waving Willows."
Who would not be transported,
In mind back to his home?[5]

This poem is entirely free of ornamentation and uses everyday words. Its completely natural expression makes it a gem of Li Bai's poetry.

From the point of view of literary criticism, the earliest instance of a stress on "Nature" comes in Liu Xie's *Carving a Dragon with a Literary Heart * On Tao, the Source*: "When we extend our observations, we find that all things, both animals and plants, have patterns of their own . . . Can these features be due to external adornment? No, they are all natural."[6] Ji Yun comments, "The literature of the Qi and Liang eras was flowery and got more ornamented and flashier by the day. Liu Xie's key point was to promote Nature as the essence of literature."[7] The chapter "Explanation of Poetry," in *Carving a Dragon with a Literary Mind* reads: "Man has seven emotions and reacts to the touch of an object. When he reacts, he chants aloud his thoughts. That is only too natural."[8] It again stresses the significance of being natural.

Following Liu Xie, Zhong Rong too was full of praise for nature. In his "Preface to Poetical Works" he says, "As for poetry, is the expression of feelings better than the quotation of classics? 'My thought of you is like the flowing water' stems from what the poet sees with his eyes; 'High platforms are prone to moaning winds' also derives from the sight; and 'Climbing to the head of an earthen bank in the morning' does not contain any literary quotation. By the same token, is the poetic sentence 'The bright moon casts its beam on the remaining snow' taken from either the *Classics* or the *Histories*? A survey of the best poems of the past and present shows that most of them are free from the practice of adding styles by quoting wantonly from the classics; instead, they have all been written depending on what the poets see and feel." He is bemoaning the addiction of contemporary writers to quotations from classical works. "Gradually it became a tradition: No sentence is without a classical quotation; no word is not taken from the classics. This affected patchwork has done severe harm to poetry. Poets who compose their poems naturally without ornamentation are really hard to come by."[9] The overuse of classical allusions obscures the natural meaning, according to Zhong Rong, and he is very much against it.

After Zhong Rong there was no shortage of upholders of nature among literary critics, like Jiao Ran of the Tang Dynasty, who said, "Happy and peaceful is literature when it directly expresses the essence of a matter, when it is strictly practical, dispenses with fancy language and is free and easy with Nature."[10] He recognized in poems such as "Recount the Virtues of Ancestors" by Xie Lingyun that "When the sun and moon are in a poem, what need is there to try to please the powerful? Hui Xiu talked about Xie's poems being like 'lotuses emerging from the water.' This indeed approaches the truth of the matter."[11] Sikong Tu, in his *Twenty-four Poems*, illustrates the meaning of "Nature" as follows: "[Poetic conception and background] do not have to be sought anywhere else; for they can be found everywhere. If a poet follows the way of Nature, he can create a poem filled with the flavor of spring. It is like flowers blooming and years passing by – all come to pass naturally. We are not going to lose what Nature gives us, but we will definitely lose what we deliberately obtain. A hermit living in the mountains is leading a life of Nature. There he enjoys a life by such things as picking an apple by chance after rain. He understands everything under the sun by way of their natural properties and lets Nature have its balanced way."[12]

Ouyang Xiu of the Song Dynasty said, "What a gentleman wants is something that will not decay, something the innermost depths of which can be descried on its surface, that is, its nature. When Yanzi (one of Confucius' disciples) lived in poverty in a back lane nobody who saw him would have thought that he would become famous down the ages. This is called seeing his nature."[13] The poet Su Shi said, "I have gone through the letters, poems and essays you sent me several times. Your works are like clouds and water drifting without fixed forms: They flow and stop as they should. Your writing is natural and your style is richly varied."[14] Fang Hui said, "A person who exercises ability can do so because he is gifted. A person who brings out the flavor of Nature can do so because he is pristine. You can have either one or the other."[15] All these people put "Nature" in the highest place.

Li Zhi of the Ming Dynasty, speaking approvingly of the heart of a child, said, "The heart of a child is a true heart. . . . For the heart of a child eschews the false and cleaves to the pure and genuine. It is the original, spontaneously aris-ing, heart."[16] What he means by the heart of a child is original human nature. To exalt the heart of a child is to exalt nature itself. When Yuan Hongdao advocates "delight," he in reality advocates "true delight." He says, "The nature of delight is deep; the study of it is shallow. If one is not conscious of delight while a child, delight will be found everywhere."[17] Only when poetry is endowed with this "true delight" can it gush spontaneously from the innermost heart. Even if there is some flaw in the composition, it will still be attractive to the readers and find wide pop-ularity. He uses the action of water as a metaphor for the "literary heart," saying that a piece of writing should flow naturally, like water; then and only then does it pass muster. His *Notes from the Hall of Literary Ripples* is an excellent discussion of this. In his critique of the *Romance of the Three Kingdoms*, Mao Zonggang of the Qing Dynasty says, "Fantasy comes unexpectedly, while technique is innate. A creator can be said to be good at literary composition. Now, when a man puts brush to paper, he must not be using fantasy here and craft there; otherwise, there would be no point in reading what a writer has in his heart when one can read what is naturally creative."[18] Yuan Mei says, "Bears' paws and panther fetuses are con-sidered the most exquisite delicacies, but if one gulps them down raw and whole they are not as delicious as ordinary vegetables and bamboo shoots. Peonies and water chestnuts are considered the most beautiful of blooms, but once they are cut and gathered they are not as attractive as wild mountain blossoms. The flavor is in the appearance, and the delight is in the essence. Once this is appreciated, a man can go on to discuss poetry."[19] Zhang Xuecheng says, "Just as the universe is reflected in Nature, so it is in men's hearts."[20] As the former gives rise to the latter, so must nature be taken as the root.

In summary, it is by grasping firmly the idea of exalting nature and the liter-ary concept of exalting the beauty of nature that we can get a fairly profound understanding of the Chinese people and Chinese literature. Of course, not all the literary figures who lauded the beauty of nature were clearly and directly influenced by the thought of Laozi and Zhuangzi; nevertheless, it cannot be denied that the root of this devotion lies in the naturalism of those two sages.

Notes

1 *Laozi*, Book 25, *Collected Works of the Philosophers*, Vol. 3, Shanghai Bookstore, 1991, P. 14
2 See *Laozi* Books 17, 23 and 51, *Collected Works of the Philosophers*, Vol. 3, Shanghai Bookstore, 1991, Pp. 10, 13, 31
3 *Laozi* Book 37, *Collected Works of the Philosophers*, Vol. 3, Shanghai Bookstore, 1991, P. 21
4 *Collected Works of Zhuangzi Interpreted * Miscellaneous Chapters * The Old Fisherman, Collected Works of the Philosophers*, Vol. 3, Shanghai Bookstore, 1991, P. 447
5 Wang Qi, annotator [Qing Dynasty]: *Complete Works of Li Taibo*, Vol. 25, Zhonghua Book Company, 1977, P. 1161
6 Fan Wenlan: *Carving a Dragon With a Literary Heart Annotated*, People's Literature Publishing House, 1978, P. 1
7 Fan Wenlan: *Carving a Dragon With a Literary Heart Annotated*, People's Literature Publishing House, 1978, P. 3
8 Fan Wenlan: *Carving a Dragon With a Literary Heart Annotated*, People's Literature Publishing House, 1978, P. 65
9 Chen Yanjie: *Poems Annotated*, People's Literature Publishing House, 1962, P. 4
10 He Wenhuan ed. [Qing Dynasty]: *Notes on Poems Through the Ages*, Zhonghua Book Company, 1981, P. 30
11 He Wenhuan ed. [Qing Dynasty]: *Notes on Poems Through the Ages*, Zhonghua Book Company, 1981, P. 30
12 He Wenhuan ed. [Qing Dynasty]: *Notes on Poems Through the Ages*, Zhonghua Book Company, 1981, P. 40
13 Ouyang Xiu [Song Dynasty]: "Inscription on the Yanghua Crag by Tang Yuanjie", *Collected Literary Works of Ouyang Xiu*, Vol. 140, *Collected Writings of the Four Basic Branches of Literature*
14 Su Shi (Su Dongpo) [Song Dynasty]: "A Reply to Xie Minshi's Letter", *Collected Works of Su Dongpo With a Short Biography*, Vol. 46, Ancient Literature Publishing House, 1957
15 Fang Hui [Yuan Dynasty]: "Preface to a Collection of Feng Botian's Poems", *Tong Jiang Collection*", Vol. 1, Jiangsu Ancient Literature Publishing House, 1988, Photocopy
16 Li Zhi [Ming Dynasty]: "Words From a Child's Heart", *Burning the Books, Poetry and Writing Collection*, Vol. 3, *Miscellaneous Accounts*, Zhonghua Book Company, 1975, P. 98
17 Yuan Hongdao [Ming Dynasty]: "A Foreword to Chen Zhengfu's *Collection of Understanding*", *Complete Works of Yuan Hongdao*, Vol. 10. Reprint of the 1829 woodblock edition by the Peiyuan Book House
18 "Reading the Annals of the Three Kingdoms", Ding Xigen ed., *Collected Prefaces and Epilogues to Chinese Novels Through the Ages*, People's Literature Publishing House, 1996, P. 923
19 Yuan Mei [Qing Dynasty]: *Talks on the Poetry of Sui Yuan*, Vol. 1, People's Literature Publishing House, 1982, P. 20
20 Zhang Xuecheng [Qing Dynasty]: *Exposition of Literary History*, privately compiled edition Part 1 *Latter Half of the Book of Changes*, Photocopy by the Cultural Relics Press of the woodblock edition of *The Literary Legacy of Mr. Zhang* by the Jia Ye Company, 1982, P. 2

Part VI

The methods and media of the transmission of Chinese literature

The transmission of literature is an important subject of literary study. Along with the development of society, the means and media of the transmission of literature also changed and became richer. This had a direct influence not only on the actual handing down of literature but also on literary creation itself. There were a variety of ways that ancient writings could be handed down, and this section can only pick out the comparatively important and meaningful ones, in fact the more representative examples, in the hope of stimulating the reader to further research.

16 Oral and performance transmission

The most ancient form of the handing down of literature was oral transmission, from mouth to ear, so to speak. It continues into our own times. Literature in remote antiquity – myths, poems and ballads – was handed down orally before it was recorded in writing. A primitive chant like "Cut bamboo and make it into a catapult; fire mud pellets and scare away wild animals" in "The Catapult Song" probably dates from the time of the Yellow Emperor, and is recorded in the book *The Spring and Autumn Annals of the Kingdoms of Wu and Yue*. Again, the "Year-end Sacrifice": "The soil turns into its dwelling; the water returns to the ditch; the insects are busy no more; and the grass and trees return to the swamp." This was a folk ballad handed down from the time of Yi Qi and is recorded in the *Book of Rites*. Again, the "Waiting for My Husband Song": "Waiting for my husband, Alas!" This song probably dates from the time Yu the Great tamed the floods. Yu's wife, a woman of the Tushan tribe, sang it as she waited for her husband to return from his irrigation work. It is recorded in the *Spring and Autumn Annals of Mr. Lv*. Whether these ballads are actually as old as this is immaterial; the important thing is that they must have existed in oral form long before they were written down. The songs recorded in the *Book of Odes* were certainly originally passed down orally before being sorted out and reduced to writing in the middle of the Spring and Autumn Period of the Zhou Dynasty. The course of oral transmission was one of unbroken refining and re-creation. It was only after the songs, poems and ballads came to be written down that they settled into a fixed form. Nevertheless, the poems and songs popular among the common people continued to be refined and reworked.

The legend of Meng Jiangnv is a typical example. This legend's origin can be traced back to the Warring States Period. The *Zuo Zhuan*, in its chapter on the 23rd year of the reign of Duke Xiang of Lu, recounts how Qi Liang dies in battle in a campaign against the State of Ju. His master, the ruler of the State of Qi, wants to hold a public mourning ceremony, but Qi Liang's widow objects, and in the end the mourning ceremony is held in the home of the deceased. Liu Xiang of the Western Han Dynasty, in his *Biographies of Old-Time Heroines*, adds a twist to this story by including an episode in which intense weeping brought the walls of a city crashing down, as follows: "Qi Liang's widow had no son. On neither the paternal nor the distaff side were there the five degrees of kinship. With no reason for returning home, she laid her head on her husband's corpse beneath the city wall [presumably of the capital of the State of Ju] and wept. Her heartbroken wailing moved passers-by to tears, and within ten days the walls of the city fell down."[1] By the time of the Northern Dynasties a major change had taken place in this story: Qi Liang had become an ordinary workman who dies helping to build the Great Wall. Weeping over her husband's body, Qi Liang's widow makes the Great Wall collapse. Later, the woman's name is revealed as Meng Jiangnv. The legend of Meng Jiangnv spread to different parts of China and in the process became mixed up with local customs and so evolved and developed. It can be found in the records of various places. In the 1920s Gu Jiegang made a systematic study of this legend, dividing the materials relating to it into "historical" and "geographical." From these two aspects, he traced the patterns of the evolution of folk legends, setting up a matrix for such studies.[2]

Another important channel for the transmission of ancient folk literature was song performances. The collections in the *Book of Odes* and the Han Dynasty Music Bureau and the folk songs of the Southern and Northern Dynasties, needless to say, could all be set to music. Besides, we have a poem by Cao Cao which goes, in part, "I climb high and recite a *fu* poem/Accompanied by flute and lyre/ It makes a separate song."[3] The story of the painted wall in the Flag Pavilion, as recounted in the *Records of Collected Oddities* by Xue Yongruo of the Tang Dynasty reveals to us the quatrain style of poetry of that dynasty. In his *Records of Escaping the Summer Heat*, Ye Mengde of the Song Dynasty tells us how common it was during that dynasty to sing *ci* poems by describing the singing of the *ci* poem "Willows for Ever" by a spring where water was drunk.[4] These are all stimulating examples of how music could be borrowed to enhance the transmission of literature.

Worthy of special attention is the use of dramatic performances to express literary works in word and gesture. Instances are the *sujiang*, a mixed ballad-song and storytelling genre of the Tang Dynasty; the storytelling and historical tales of the Song and Yuan Dynasties and the dramas and Southern Opera of the Yuan Dynasty. These, together with later opera and music styles, of which many had no script to rely on but were passed down orally from master to apprentice, were gradually organized into forms in which they were later recorded. These works, from the Song Dynasty on, formed a corpus of a great literary heritage which at times occupied a more important position in Chinese literature than poetry.

These two methods of transmission – oral and written – often complemented and promoted each other. To illustrate this, let us examine how the *Romance of the Three Kingdoms* came to be compiled in book form. The original rich and varied stories of the three kingdoms (Shu, Wei and Wu) were contained in a book titled, *Annals of the Three Kingdoms*, with a commentary by Pei Song. These stories quite early on became part of the folk tradition. In his *Reminiscences of the Da Ye Reign Period* (605–617), Du Bao describes how Emperor Yang of the Sui Dynasty watched a performance given on a pond, which consisted of stories from the Three Kingdoms tradition. Among the Song Dynasty storytelling items there was a "Story in Three Parts," and in the Zhizhi reign period of Yuan Emperor

Yingzong was published the *Annals of the Three Kingdoms in Plain Language*. In his *Records of Ceasing to Plow in South Village*, Tao Zongyi includes several stories from the Three Kingdoms, including the *Decisive Battle at the Red Cliff*, in the list of operas in his Golden Courtyard repertoire. From this we can deduce that a large number of operas and plays with Three Kingdoms stories as their themes were common on the stage during the Jin and Yuan Dynasties. Luo Guanzhong's famous *Romance of the Three Kingdoms* was based on the *Annals of the Three Kingdoms* with Pei Song's commentary, but it also drew on various accounts handed down in spoken or sung form as public performances. It was on this basis that the book was arranged, refined and completed. Moreover, after the appearance of the completed *Romance of the Three Kingdoms* more literary performances of stories connected with the Three Kingdoms appeared, and vigor was injected into both the storytellers and stage performances.

Oral transmission and performance were of course important forms of the transmission of literature since ancient times, but in the course of its being handed down, unless it was put into writing in time, there was a very real danger of oral literature being lost. Some of the myths recorded in the ancient work known as the *Classic of Mountains and Seas* are preserved only in very sketchy form, whereas it is thought that originally they were much more elaborate, and it is a great pity that much has been lost. From the *Zuo Zhuan*, we know that in the *Book of Odes* there were originally more poems and songs than the 305 now extant, one of which was titled, "River Water." According to the *History of the Han Dynasty * Records of Art and Literature*, there were 314 volumes of poems and songs compiled during the Western Han Dynasty, mainly in the collection of the Music Bureau. But nowadays only about 50 or so poems and songs survive that can be positively identified as having been in the Western Han's Music Bureau files. The others have all been lost. We have no way of calculating how many precious items of literature have perished in the process of being transmitted orally during the several thousand years of Chinese history. And so we must value even more highly the literary heritage that has been passed down us, make more efforts to salvage such items of literature, and preserve, arrange and record them.

Notes

1 Liu Xiang [Han Dynasty]: *Biographies of Old-Time Heroines*, Vol. 4, *Collected Writings of the Four Basic Branches of Literature*
2 Gu Jiegang ed.: *Studies on Stories About Meng Jiangnv*, 3 volumes in total, Institute of Philology and History of National Sun Yat-sen University, 1928
3 Xiao Yi [Liang Dynasty, Southern Dynasties Period]: *The Golden Tower*, Vol.1, *Collected Works From Lack of Knowledge Studio*, Vol. 9, woodblock print, sixth year (1826) of the Daoguang reign period of the Qing Dynasty
4 The original text is "Out for a stroll, Yu Shidan chanced to see an official who has forsaken the Western Xia, and said, 'Wherever there is a well for drinking water the Willow Ci can be heard.'"

17 The invention of paper, copying, inscriptions and seeking preferment

Before the invention of paper, words were inscribed on such materials as tortoise shells or bones, metal or stone, bamboo strips or silk. An example is an inscription on a stone drum excavated in the early Tang Dynasty at Tianxing (present-day Baoji City in Shaanxi Province). Carved on 10 faces of the drum is a lively poem about hunting. Studies have dated it to the early years of the State of Qin during the Eastern Zhou Period (770–256 BC). During the Xiping reign period (172–178) of Emperor Ling of the Eastern Han Dynasty a stone pillar was set up in front of the main gate of the National Academy bearing seven inscriptions from the Confucian classics as the standard texts. Cai Yong and some others came up with the idea of engraving the seven volumes of the Confucius classics on stone. Cai himself wrote them on the pillar in the clerical-script style. The *History of the Later Han Dynasty * Biography of Cai Yong* reads: During the fourth year of the Xiping reign period, Cai Yong "pleaded with the Ling emperor to allow him to proofread and correct the errors found in the 'Six Confucius Classics,' and the latter gave him his consent. Cai then inscribed the Confucian texts on a stone tablet with ink of cinnabar and hired a mason to engrave them on it. After it was finished, he had the tablet erected in front of the National Academy's main gate. Confucian scholars and students of the later generations all used the engraved texts as the standard. When the tablet was first erected, viewers and those who wanted to copy the texts came by more than a thousand chariot-loads a day, so much so that they jammed the streets all around."[1] *Jian-du* was made of either bamboo or wood whittled and pared down to slips. Bamboo slips were called "jian" and wood "du." Texts were written on them with a brush pen soaked with ink. A number of slips were strung into a book known as "ce." Large amounts of *jian-du ce* have been excavated in Dunhuang and Juyan, as well as Shangcha of Hunan, Jiangling of Hubei and Linyi of Shandong. Before the invention of paper, most of the ancient classics had been recorded on bamboo or wood slips and survive to this day.

Nevertheless, the disadvantages of the above-mentioned materials were only too apparent: They were too hard to engrave, too cumbersome to transport or too expensive to own. Therefore they presented a hindrance to the promulgation of literature. The emergence of paper eliminated those disadvantages. Made of tree bark, bits of hemp ropes and cloth as well as used fishing nets, paper was less costly and could be rolled up and folded out. Being so portable, it was the best material for writing and thus became the ideal media of popularizing literary works.

When exactly paper was invented is still a moot question among academic circles. In any event, all agree that the improvement on the technique of manufacturing paper made by Cai Lun, a eunuch of the Eastern Han Dynasty, was a significant event in the history of Chinese civilization. Paper had in fact been available before his time. Some archeologists point out that the earliest paper ever discovered is the piece unearthed in 1986 from the Western Han tomb in Fangmatan, Tianshui City, Gansu Province. The paper bears something like a map painted with mountains, ravines, rivers and streets.

It had taken a long time, however, for paper to be popularly used since its invention. For a large part of the period between Eastern Han and the early Six Dynasties, bamboo and wood slips were still the dominant media for writing. Evidence for this turned up in 1996, when a large quantity of such strips from the Kingdom of Wu (of the Three Kingdoms Period) was excavated at Zoumalou, Changsha, Hunan Province. As for silk as a writing medium, the *Biography of Suo Jing*, Volume 60 of the *History of the Jin Dynasty*, refers to Suo Jing's "'Running Hand' Style of Calligraphy" as follows: "His masterpieces written on fine silk would stand out for one hundred generations."[2]

But from the time of the Western Jin Dynasty paper became the predominant medium for writing. Pan Yue, in his "A Preface to the Poetic Exposition Expressing My Feelings in the Autumn," talks about "gathering together writing materials and paper, and then with great effort composing a *fu* poem."[3] Shi Chong, in his "Poems Before I Die," says, "I grasp the paper, and my five senses are clogged. I wield the writing brush, and words come pouring out."[4] Fu Xian of the Western Jin Dynasty says in his "*Fu* Poems Written on Paper": "There have always been plainness and colorfulness in the world, and gains and losses in the operation of governance. Therefore, the rites must change in accordance with the times, and vessels with the objects they contain. Record-keeping by way of tying knots gave way to the oracle-bone script. Then paper was invented to create books. As convenient as silk, it is the result of change. Paper is as valuable as silk, for it is regular, clean and pliable in nature. Boasting the capacity to carry articles in exquisite language, it is really good for literature. Paper is a brand-new product made of unpromising materials. Pull it, and it opens; let it go, and it rolls up. Therefore, it can be bent and extended, opened and closed."[5] We can see how people at that time delighted in and valued paper. The use of paper by literary figures grew by leaps and bounds after the Western Jin Dynasty. In his "Preface to the Twenty Drinking Wine Poems," Tao Yuanming says, "After getting drunk I amuse myself with a few verses. There is plenty of paper and ink, but the words don't come out in the right order." In his poem "Chiding Sons" he says, "Although there are five fellows, they have no love for the paper and writing brush." By the time of the Tang Dynasty paper was being universally used for writing on. More evidence comes from the paper manuscripts of all kinds discovered in caves at Dunhuang, including transcripts of literary works such as *Selected Works of*

Literature. Transcriptions of Tang literary works were not only widespread, they were also sold as commercial items. In his "Preface to *The Changqing Collection about a Woman with the Name Bai*," Yuan Zhen says,

> For twenty years now, in the imperial palaces, in government offices, in Taoist and Buddhist temples, in courier stations and even upon the very walls there are writings. Wherever there are princes, concubines and boys herding oxen – and even where horses go, everywhere you can find them. Hand-copied and block-printed [Tang poems] sell like hot cakes in the market, and are even accepted in payment for choice wines and teas. Writings even announce the names of robbers, advertise goods for sale and plaster the walls of privies. It's a hopeless situation . . . There is even a story that merchants from Silla have said that their prime minister is willing to give one hundred pieces of gold for a book, but he can instantly detect a fake. There has never been such a widespread flow of writings.[6]

Bai Xingjian of the mid-Tang Dynasty, in his *The Story of Li Wa*, says that after Li Wa took in Rong Yangsheng, who had been a beggar, "she ordered a carriage to go out. Rong Yangsheng followed behind on horseback. Upon reaching a bookshop by the south gate of the Flag Pavilion, Li Wa allowed Rong Yangsheng to choose books, which she then bought for a total of 100 pieces of gold. With the purchases loaded, the pair returned."[7] From this short anecdote we can get a glimpse of the book business at that time: Chang'an [the capital of the Tang Dynasty] had a specialized book market, with a multitude of titles to choose from. Moreover, for one customer to spend 100 pieces of gold on books is evidence that this was not a petty business. These expensive books would, of course, have been hand-copied.

The universal use of paper made books both easy to write and easy to distribute. It also gave writers more opportunities to study each other's works and to gather together. All this had a deep and wide impact on literary creation and research. There was a veritable explosion of writers and their works from the Western Jin Dynasty on, and we have to recognize that this was closely connected with the use of paper, as was the advent of middle- and lower-ranking scholars to the literary stage.

Another form of literary transmission was writing poems on paintings. Inscribed poems in fact became an inseparable part of paintings, and such paintings formed a distinct branch of art. Emperor Kangxi of the Qing Dynasty included over 8,900 poems inscribed on paintings in a work on the subject in 120 volumes. And even this considerable number did not exhaust the genre. The more famous earlier poems inscribed on paintings include "Poem to Add to the Distinguished Chamberlain Zhao Yan's Pastel Painting" by Li Bai and "Poem to Add Jokingly to Wang Zai's Landscape Painting" by Du Fu, both of the Tang Dynasty. These are regarded as superb examples. A later couplet goes, "The influence of a fine work surpasses anything in ancient times/It may be near at hand, but it deserves to be discussed for 10,000 li." From this we can see in what high esteem painting was held.

Another method of literary transmission worthy of notice, and a very interesting one at that, is that of inscriptions on walls. That wall inscriptions started before the Tang Dynasty we can deduce from the *History of the Liang Dynasty * Biography of Emperor Jianwen*, which says, "In imprisonment, [he] inscribed his own preface."[8] However, this genre really came into its own during the Tang Dynasty. We find in the *An Old History of the Tang Dynasty * Biography of Wang Ji* the following: "Wang Ji often wrote verses on walls, usually satirizing do-gooders."[9] According to the *Complete Tang Poems*, there were several thousand wall poems at that time, and according to the *Complete Song Poems* over 10,000.

Wall poems could be found in many places – in scenic and tourist spots such as temples and pavilions, in government offices, post stations and places of entertainment, and in one's own or a friend's house. An interesting example is a poem that a Tang Dynasty prime minister wrote on a wall of his office in praise of one Wang Wan, titled, "Lingering at the Foot of Mount Beigu." Included are the lines, "The daily dawn dispels the shreds of night/The river banishes the old year with the spring," and "Every display of your literary skill/Is couched in an exquisite pattern."[10] Of the leading Tang poets who wrote wall poems we can cite Wang Bo's "A Wall-Inscribed Poem in Jianyin, Pu'an," Cen Shen's "A Poem Inscribed on Chamberlain Wei's Hall Wall in Yongle," Bai Juyi's "A Poem Inspired by an Accidental Visit with Liu Yuxi to Cui Qun's House," Bao Ji's "A Poem Inscribed Jokingly on the Office Wall of the Judges" and Lv Yan's "A Poem Inscribed on the Wall of a Brothel in the Capital." Of the Song Dynasty poets, Kou Zhun wrote "Inscribed in a Pavilion by the River," Wang Anshi wrote "To a Friend," Li Peng wrote "Returning to My Study from Yuzhang," Fang Yue wrote "Getting Drunk in My Farm Cottage on the Right When Rain Stops the Day's Plowing" and Lu You wrote "Mountain Home." There were also wall poems written in the same meter or style in reply to previous ones, such as Quan Deyu's "A Poem to Echo Chamberlain Wei's Wall-Inscribed Long Poem at the Time When the Roses Blossomed at General Congshu's House."

There are many stories connected with the wall poems. In his *Talks in the Garden of Ci Poems*, Xu Gui says, "In the *Night Words of the Cold Studio* it says, 'Before the poet Su Dongpo got acquainted with Shao You, the latter learned that Su Dongpo was about to pass through Weiyang, and so he wrote a poem on a wall in a mountain monastery, in imitation of the poet's style. Su Dongpo, of course did not recognize it, and was very surprised. Later, he went to see Sun Shenlao, who showed him some of Shao You's poems and *ci* compositions. Reading them, Su Dongpo gasped in astonishment, exclaiming, "So he was the one who wrote that poem on the wall!"[11] But the most famous story is the one about Li Bai mounting the Yellow Crane Tower. This story is contained in the *Biographies of Talented Persons of the Tang Dynasty*, Volume 1 "Biography of Cui Hao": "Afterwards [Cui Hao] visited Wuchang, where he mounted the Yellow Crane Tower. He composed a *fu* poem there, and wrote it on a wall. When Li Bai arrived at the same spot, he said, 'I cannot express in words the beauty of the scenery; Cui Hao's inscribed poem cannot be bettered.'" Leaving without writing a word means that the great master of poetry refrains from acting rashly. In the *Records of Tang*

Poetry Volume 21 it says, "When Li Bai saw the poem Cui Hao had inscribed on a wall of the Yellow Crane Tower he forthwith composed the 'Phoenix Terrace Verses' to try to match it."[12] Scenic spots like the Yellow Crane Tower were the sort of places where literary figures were inspired to inscribe poems on walls, examples of which can be found today on the China Daily BBS website.

Among the scholars of the Tang Dynasty it was fashionable to compete for preferment and in this way to win an influential reputation and high social standing, and so increase their chances of promotion. Poems, including those in the *ci* and *fu* styles, were often used as means of gaining favor with superiors. For instance, Wang Wei's "Offered to Prince Zhang Ling" and "Dedicated to Prince Shi Xing" were attempts to gain favor with the senior official Zhang Jiuling; Li Bai's "For Han Jingzhou" served a similar function vis-à-vis Han Chaozong; Du Fu's *fu* poems "Morning Offering to the Taiqing Palace," "Morning Rite at the Ancestral Shrine" and "Business in the Southern Suburbs" were all offered to emperors. Such poems, aimed at using literary works to gain personal advancement, were all written with meticulous care and so can be regarded as another channel for the transmission of literature. Looking at such poems with a candid eye, we can say that they widen the scope of the handing down of literature.

Notes

1 Fan Hua [Song Dynasty, Southern Dynasties Period]: *History of the Later Han Dynasty*, Vol.60, Part 2, Zhonghua Book Company, 1965, P. 1990

2 Fang Xuanling et al. [Tang Dynasty]: *History of the Jin Dynasty*, Vol. 60, Zhonghua Book Company, 1974, P. 1649

3 Li Shan, Lv Yanji et al. [Tang Dynasty]: *Selection of the Literary Works of Six Officials*, Vol. 13, *Collected Writings of the Four Basic Branches of Literature*

4 Li Shan, Lv Yanji et al. [Tang Dynasty]: *Selection of the Literary Works of Six Officials*, Vol. 23, *Collected Writings of the Four Basic Branches of Literature*

5 Ouyang Xun et al. eds. [Tang Dynasty]: *Comprehensive Categories of Art and Literature*, Vol. 58, Shanghai Ancient Books Publishing House, 1982, P. 1053

6 Zhu Jincheng: *Collected Works of Bai Juyi With Notes*, Shanghai Ancient Books Publishing House, 1988, P. 3972

7 Li Shiren: *Complete Novels of the Tang and Five Dynasties Periods*, Shaanxi People's Publishing House, 1998, P. 630

8 Yao Silian [Tang Dynasty]: *History of the Liang Dynasty*, Vol. 4, Zhonghua Book Company, 1973, P. 108

9 Liu Yun et al. *An Old History of the Tang Dynasty*, Vol. 192, Zhonghua Book Company, 1975, P. 5116

10 See *Collection of Martyrs of Rivers and Mountains*, commentary, *Selection of Tang Poetry by Tang Scholars*, Zhonghua Book Company, 1958, P. 106

11 Tang Guizhang (annotator): *Talks in the Garden of Ci Poems*, Vol. 10, Shanghai Ancient Books Publishing House, 1981, P. 220

12 Fu Xuanzong (chief ed.): *Accounts of the Talented Persons of the Tang Dynasty With Notes*, Vol. 1, Zhonghua Book Company, 1987, P. 202

18 The invention of printing and the diffusion of literary works

The first books to emerge with the invention of printing in the Tang Dynasty were works of history and the Buddhist scriptures. Examples are a history book printed by the Pan Shang Press of Chengdu and the *Usnisa Vijaya Dharani Sutra* printed by the Longchi Fangbian Press.[1] In the Song Dynasty the printing of books had spread much further afield than in the Tang and Five Dynasties periods, and the subject matter of the books had expanded too. There was a veritable forest of bookshops in the Song Dynasty capital alone. Apart from Buddhist scriptures, collections of the works of the masters of the classics and history were printed, as well as books of popular and recreational literature.

With the development of printing from the Song Dynasty, the printing of books gradually became universal (as opposed to hand-copying), and the number of bookstores in the urban markets increased. Even during the Song Dynasty anecdotes concerning bookstores abounded. In the 10th volume of his "Epilogue to Ancient Records," Ouyang Xiu says, "A copy of the highly esteemed *The Yellow Court Classic* was later acquired from a bookstore in the capital." And in his *Discussions of Old Man Gui's Poetry*, Volume 3 of his *Reminiscences About Reading Books in the Prefectural Studio*, he says, "Toward the end of the Xuanhe reign period (1119–1126) there were businesses in the capital that both printed and sold books." Jiang Xiaoyu, in Volume 36 of his *Garden of Factual Things*, says, "One day, I came across some poems by Feng Yingwang in the Xiangguo Temple bookstore. I read a few, then went back." The bookstores were not confined to the capital, however; there were establishments that printed and published books in other areas too. In his "Books Compiled by the Yang Company," Volume 9 of his *Remembrances of Kui Tan*, Yue Ke says, "The Jianyang Bookstore compiled publications and issued them at different times, daily or monthly, and they were quickly on sale all over Hebei Province, disseminating knowledge far and wide."[2] From the Yuan Dynasty on, the book printing and selling business burgeoned much more than it had in the Song Dynasty, and the booksellers dealt with a lot more popular reading matter. In the Zhizhi reign period of Emperor Yingzong of Yuan, the Jian An Yu Company published *The Five Kinds of Illustrated Vernacular Fictions*, and in the first year (1522) of the Jiajing reign period of Emperor Shizong of the Ming Dynasty it published the *Romance of the Three Kingdoms in Popular Language* in 24 volumes.

With the development of the art of printing and books and bookstores becoming the new dominant medium of the transmission of literature, great strides were made in literary creation. Moreover, there was a great surge in the number of poets who became scholars and scholars who were at the same time poets. In the Tang Dynasty an accomplished scholar "who had read 10,000 books" (Du Fu: "A Letter of Twenty-Two Rhymed Lines Respectfully Dedicated to Mr. Wei, Assistant Director of the Left in the Department of State Affairs") was a rarity, but in the Song Dynasty it was quite easy to find such persons. Song Dynasty scholars "expressed their writings in the form of poetry, their learning in the form of poetry and their discussions in the form of poetry."[3] This new situation had a very close connection with the expansion of knowledge in the wake of the widespread dissemination of books.

Even more noteworthy is the fact that, following the geographical expansion of the art of printing, from the Yuan Dynasty on a great number of literary works of the popular kind were printed, and this, coupled with the comparatively low cost of publishing, was an important factor in the rapid expansion of the popularity of novels, local operas and all kinds of dramatic works. In addition, the publication of a large number of works with illustrations, including illustrated popular literature, served as a new source of strength for the dissemination of literature. The value of these printed materials was already attracting wide-ranging attention, and as time went on it became an even more important topic.

Notes

1 Refer to Zhang Xiumin: *The Invention of Printing in China and Its Influence*, People's Publishing House, 1958, P. 63
2 Yue Ke [Song Dynasty]: *Remembrances of Kui Tan*, Vol. 9, *First Edition of the Collected Literary Works*
3 Yan Yu [Song Dynasty]: *Canglang's Remarks on Poetry*, Vol. 1, People's Literature Publishing House, 1961, P. 24

Part VII

Appreciation of Chinese literature

19 Taste

The word "appreciation" in its ancient usage meant "recognize the worth of." In recent times its meaning has been expanded, and what we nowadays call "appreciation of literature" was in ancient times expressed by several other collocations, meaning "ponder" or "enjoy reciting." In *New Words for the World * Ren Dan* we find: "Liu Yin (Tan) said, 'Sun Chenggong, the Crazy Scholar, whenever he went somewhere, would spend a few days in appreciation [the word used is "enjoy"]; if he couldn't do that, he would turn back halfway along the road.'"[1] The *Annals of the Three Kingdoms * Section on the Kingdom of Wei, Biography of Wang Can* cites the *Annals of the State of Wei* to say, "Ji Kang wrote essays totaling 60,000 to 700,000 words, all of them for enjoyable recitation."[2] By "enjoyable recitation" here is meant recreational reading plus reading out loud for oneself or others to enjoy. Su Dongpo says in his "Written After Wang Gong Carved a Poem on a Wall of a Gorge," the third part of *Postscript to Su Dongpo's Works*: "Wang Gong carved a poem in Taiwei Gorge. Reading it several times for pleasure there arise stark and clear before one's eyes ruddy armor, white salt, the Yanyu Rock and the shapes of tawny oxen."[3] Here the word used for "reading" implies internal gratification as one absorbs the meaning of the verses. The character meaning "play" is present in all these expressions, but this does not mean that a work of literature should be read in a flippant or careless manner. Whatever the subject, if the work does not lead the reader into a transcendental world, it cannot be described using the word for "play" in any of its various collocations. If this transcendental world is meant, then it would be easy simply to add the words "understand" or "penetrate" before "play." If, when one reads a literary work, one finds it a chore, and not "play" in any sense of the word, then one feels as though facing a test or being forced to find the substance in the work; in any case one can not be said to be truly understanding the text. Only when the reader can both fully understand the work and truly enjoy it, with these two aspects reinforcing each other, can such a work boast a high level of accomplishment. *Carving a Dragon with a Literary Heart * Knowing Sounds* deals with literary appreciation. It contains the phrase "playing with the meaning," which really means "seeking inspiration from a study of the meaning." A whole new understanding comes about from the juxtaposition of the words "play" and "meaning."

The character "wei," meaning "taste," which occurs in some of these "appreciation" expressions, is also worthy of note. Basically it means the sensation at the end of the tongue, and this was extended to convey the idea of savoring the flavor of a literary work, or "appreciating" it. Lu Ji, in his "Rhapsody on Literature," says, "It is as if it tasted like the flavor of a meat soup with no spices added to it or as if it were a monotonous tune played on a zither."[4] In the chapter "Explanation of Poetry" in *Carving a Dragon with a Literary Heart* we find, "In Zhang Heng's 'Complaint' there are fine classics for the tasting."[5] Again, in the "Emotion and Literary Grace" we find "An article written in flowery language but lacking content must be insipid to its readers."[6] All these instances include the character for "taste." The book *Poetical Works* stresses taste, and in its preface says, "With concepts loftier than the words, they are bland and tasteless"; "A poem with five characters to a line plays an important role in poetry and is therefore considered the most interesting of all forms of poetry" and "It gives those who appreciate it a lasting and pleasant aftertaste, and constantly moves those who listen to it. Such is the ideal form of poetry."[7] Zhong Rong discusses what an "insipid taste" is; he also discusses what means by its opposite, which he calls "limitless," meaning a rich and everlasting flavor; in other words, while the actual matter of a literary work is necessarily limited, as is its content, its "flavor" should be without limit. What is called "appreciation" is the savoring of the "taste" of a literary work both within and outside the actual words used. Sikong Tu, a late-Tang poetry critic, in his "A Discussion of Poetry Dedicated to Li Sheng," says, "There have been many explanations in both ancient and modern times of what comprises poetry. It is foolish to simply say that poetry is something that has a flavor. South of Jiangling the people are very particular about taste: If something is pickled it is also bitter, and is considered bitter and nothing more; if it is vinegary, it is also salty, and is considered salty and nothing more. If people used to luxurious living are suddenly faced with starvation all food is delicious to them even though they know that there are more tastes than just salty and bitter ones."[8] Sikong Tu's discussion of "taste" is aimed at appreciation of the exquisite flavors that exist in literature outside the salty and bitter ones. Only when one can ruminate on a literary work can one be said to "appreciate" it, and someone good at ruminating in this way was also good at appreciating literature. This was the traditional Chinese viewpoint on literary appreciation.

Literature is an art of words, and literary appreciation is above all a pondering of words. The first step is to understand what one reads, but this alone is far from enough; one must be able to grasp the subtleties and beauty of the words, mull them over and ponder them deeply. In China there is a saying, as follows: "Gnaw the text and chew the words." This has a somewhat derogatory meaning, as it implies shallow nit-picking, but the same attitude is indispensable for literary appreciation. In his "Thesis in Verse Dedicated to Court Official Zhang Zhongjie," Yuan Yishan says, "A piece of writing should be accomplished one character at a time, and it should be read one character at a time. So long as there is any flavor untasted, one hundred readings are not enough."[9] This is an expression of true experience of literary appreciation.

To grasp the words it is first of all necessary to recognize that the definitions in dictionaries, thesauruses and phrase books cannot convey the flavor of the writing to the reader. Moreover, the notes to a text in general do no more than explain the meaning of a phrase or an allusion. The resonance hidden deeply in the words, in conjunction with their surface coloring, cannot be construed by recourse to reference works or notes alone; only through a great amount of reading and repeated pondering can the deep-down meaning gradually be absorbed. For example:

The phrase "bai ri," literally "white sun," would be simply be reproduced as "sun" in a dictionary of phrases, but anybody steeped in ancient poetry would know that the character for "sun" preceded by that for "white" to describe the sun's brightness would refer to a certain type of weather. According to Zuo Si: "A shining sun in a brilliantly clear sky bathes the whole of China in light."[10] Bao Zhao says, "When a shining sun lies overhead, the whole world is illuminated."[11] So a "bai ri" is not simply a sun: It signifies brilliant light as far as the eye can see. Wang Zhihuan's "Ascending the Stork Tower" starts with "All the mountains are bathed in brilliant sunshine."[12] In fact, even when an evening or a sunset is described using these two characters the sight conjured up by the reader is of a shiningly brilliant landscape.

Again, we have "lu chuang," which literally means a "green-colored screen window." However, in poetic language it means, figuratively, a cozy home atmosphere. In his "Night Moon," Liu Fangping says,

> Tonight I incline my head,
> To sense the warm breath of spring.
> The chirping of the insects,
> Comes newly through the green screen window.[13]

Wen Tingyun, in his "Pusaman" says,

> The leaves fall and the cuckoos call,
> A green screen window in my reverie.[14]

Wei Zhuang says in his "Pusaman" says,

> They urge me to hurry away home,
> To the flower-like people of my green windows.[15]

These are all examples of the real meaning of "lu chuang."

"Ban qiao" literally means a plank bridge, but it has an extended poetic meaning as compared to "wooden bridge." In his "Yangliuzhi (Willow Branches)," Liu Yuxi says,

> On the river in springtime,
> Countless crooked willow branches.
> Twenty years ago on the old wooden bridge,

My love and I parted.
And, alas, still no news of her.[16]

Wen Tingyun, in his "A Morning Stroll on Mount Shang," says, "I hear the cock crow in the thatched cottage under the moon/I see footprints on the frost-covered plank bridge."[17] To substitute "wooden" for "plank" would lose the poetic flavor of the original. Wood only means the material out of which the bridge was made, whereas "plank" has imagery clinging to it.

"Eastern fence" in Tao Yuanming's "Drinking Wine" is another example. In this poem he says, "Picking chrysanthemums below the eastern fence/I gaze at the southern mountains far away."[18] There was in fact a fence around the eastern side of his courtyard, and chrysanthemums did indeed grow there. But because Tao Yuanming was a noted recluse, the chrysanthemum became a virtual embodiment of himself, and the "eastern fence" a symbol of distance from the sordid world.

Let us take a look at Du Fu's poem, "Coming Across a Disfavored Court Musician on the Southern Shore of the Yangtze River":

How oft in princely mansions did we meet!
As oft in lordly halls I heard you sing.
Now the southern scenery is most sweet,
But I meet you again in parting spring.[19]

"The season of falling blossoms" refers to a definite time of the year. But it also has the recondite meanings of the chance meeting between the poet and Li Guinian and the situation at the Tang Dynasty court at that time. In this sense the expression provides much food for thought.

The works of the pre-Qin philosophers also contain many phrases with multiple layers of meaning. In the "There Is Yong" section of the *Analects* we find "Bo Niu being ill, the Master went to ask for him. He took hold of his hand through the window, and said, 'It is killing him. It is the appointment of Heaven, alas! That such a man should have such a sickness! That such a man should have such a sickness!'"[20] The repetition of the phrase "such a man" adequately conveys Confucius' feeling of compassion for Bo Niu.

New Words for the World contains some lively discourses of famous scholars. In the section titled, "Literature," the words "without making the slightest progress" are very expressive of feeling:

Zhi Daolin stayed in the Dong'an Temple after he first came to Jiankang from Huiji. Secretary Wang came to chat with him, thinking that he was well prepared for a conversation with sophisticated argumentation and brilliant rhetoric. Unfortunately, he found himself no match for Zhi Daolin. The secretary had thought that his lengthy speech or article was full of sagacious reasoning and florid language, but Zhi said unhurriedly: "In the long time since we last met you have made no progress either in argumentation or in the use of words." Ashamed, Secretary Wang left.[21]

Novels and dramas also contain phrases with such deep allusions – for instance, "yellow soup," which occurs in Chapter 44 of *A Dream of Red Mansions*. Lady Dowager cursed Jia Lian: "You degenerate! After drinking the yellow soup you might at least stretch out on your bed quietly like a corpse instead of beating your wife."[22] Here "yellow soup" is a pejorative term for wine, which was usually of a yellow color. Again, in Chapter 14 of *Outlaws of the Marsh* we find "You brute! Instead of coming to see me you swig the yellow stuff on the street. Don't I have enough wine for you? You really put me to shame!"[23] In the Yuan Dynasty poetic drama *The Cinnabar Burden* occurs the following: "I've drunk too many bowls of that yellow soup to catch up with him." When cursing a drunkard the phrase "yellow soup, not "yellow wine" is used. Similarly, the phrase "stiff corpse" is used pejoratively about someone sleeping. This crops up in the 12th chapter of *Traces of the Flowery Moon*: "You must have been drunk to come here kicking the door down, and then stretching out without a word, like a corpse. Frightening the life out of people!"[24] The scornful attitude is clear in both phrases "yellow soup" and "stiff corpse."

"Mouthless gourd" is an epithet for a man of few words. The gourd recalls a man with a simple and honest nature, and by adding "mouthless" to the image of a gourd the image comes out more strongly and is worth pondering over. In *A Dream of Red Mansions* Chapter 78 we find, "Xi Ren has from childhood been taciturn, what I would call a 'mouthless gourd.' Since you knew that, how could you make such a big mistake?"[25] And in Chapter 38 of *Journey to the West*: "Even if he were a calabash without a mouth, he would roll back and forth to harass you so you can't do anything about him."[26] Again, in the second act of the Yuan Dynasty poetic drama *The Butterfly Dream*: "Even if he were all mouth, he would not make excuses, but in fact he's just like a mouthless gourd."[27]

In Chapter 7 of *A Dream of Red Mansions*, when Bao Yu meets Qin Zhong, Qin Keqing's younger brother, for the first time, Big Sister Phoenix insists on meeting Qin Zhong also. When Qin Zhong bows to and greets Big Sister Phoenix, the latter says, smiling: "'You two are so alike!' She bent down to take the child by the hand, and told him to sit beside her."[28] Her comparison is very vivid, inasmuch as it conveys not only the delight of Big Sister Phoenix at meeting Qin Zhong, but also her affection for Bao Yu. For in fact Big Sister Phoenix is always comparing other people to Bao Yu and finding that none of them come up to his standard – until this episode, when she remarks that Qin Zhong and Bao Yu are alike. Immediately the image and voice of a rather shrewish girl appears before the reader's eyes.

In Chapter 3 of *Outlaws of the Marsh*, there is a scene in which Lu Tixia beats Zhen Guanxi: "Hearing this, he leapt to his feet. Seizing the bundles of mincemeat one in each hand, he glared at Zheng the Butcher, and roared, 'I'll give you something to chortle about!' And he thrust the two bundles of mincemeat in the other's face, and commenced giving him a thorough drubbing." The phrase used to describe the "thorough drubbing" is "meat rain." Over this, Jin Sheng sighed in admiration: "An all-time masterpiece of writing!" In Li Zhaowu's opinion, "meat rain" is a "most apt and unsurpassed description." Yuan Wuwa's comment was

"The phrase "meat rain" is a common but at the same time refined description. Intriguing, it quite describes blows from fists falling like raindrops."[29]

Literature is an art of words, and literary creation cannot dispense with words as its tools. However, the descriptive power of words is limited. Even a master wordsmith will come across headaches in verbal expression from time to time. China's literary figures well knew the truth that "words cannot do full justice to meaning," and so they have tended to pay more attention to the inspirational and covert aspects of words to express the subtle flavor of their writings outside the words themselves. This has resulted in a pursuit of unbounded meaning free from the limits of language. The appreciation of Chinese literature must of course begin with the language, but by no means should it be restricted by the language. It should progress from within the words to outside the words, and taste the flavor lingering between the lines. This is one key to appreciating Chinese literature.

Notes

1 Liu Yiqing [Song Dynasty of the Southern Dynasties Period]: *New Words for the World*, Shanghai Ancient Books Publishing House, 1982, photocopy of the Sixian Jiangshe woodblock edition, 1891

2 Chen Shou [Western Jin Dynasty]: *Annals of the Three Kingdoms*, Vol. 21, Zhonghua Book Company, 1974, P. 606

3 *Collected Works of Su Shi*, Vol. 68, Zhonghua Book Company, 1986, P. 3159

4 Li Shan, Lv Yanji et al. [Tang Dynasty]: *Selection of the Literary Works of Six Officials*, Vol.17, *Collected Writings of the Four Basic Branches of Literature*

5 Fan Wenlan: *Carving a Dragon With a Literary Heart Annotated*, Vol. 2, People's Literature Publishing House, 1978, P. 66

6 Fan Wenlan: *Carving a Dragon With a Literary Heart Annotated*, Vol. 7, People's Literature Publishing House, 1978, P. 539

7 Chen Yanjie: *Poems Annotated*, People's Literature Publishing House, 1962, PP. 1, 2

8 *Collected Works Extolling the Sages by the Minister of Works*, Vol. 2, *Collected Writings of the Four Basic Branches of Literature*

9 Shi Guoqi [Qing Dynasty]: *Collected Poems of Yuan Yishan With Commentary and Notes*, Vol.2, People's Literature Publishing House, 1985, P. 122

10 Zuo Si [Jin Dynasty]: "Singing of History", No. 5 *Poems of the Pre-Qin, Han, Wei, Jin, and Northern and Southern Dynasties* compiled and checked by Lu Qinli, Zhonghua Book Company, 1983, P. 733

11 Bao Zhao [Song Dynasty, Southern Dynasties Period]: The fifth of the "Five Poems Imitating the Style of Liu Gonggan", *Poems of the Pre-Qin, Han, Wei, Jin, and Northern and Southern Dynasties* compiled and checked by Lu Qinli, Zhonghua Book Company, 1983, P. 1299

12 *Complete Tang Poems*, Vol. 253, Zhonghua Book Company, 1960, P. 2849

13 *Complete Tang Poems*, Vol. 251, Zhonghua Book Company, 1960, P. 2840

14 Li Yimang: *Collected Teachings Among the Flowers*, People's Literature Publishing House, 1958, P. 3

15 Li Yimang: *Collected Teachings Among the Flowers*, People's Literature Publishing House, 1958, P. 31

16 *Complete Tang Poems*, Vol. 365, Zhonghua Book Company, 1960, P. 4129

17 *Complete Tang Poems*, Vol. 581, Zhonghua Book Company, 1960, P. 6741

18 "Drinking Wine", No. 5 *Collected Works of Tao Yuanming Annotated*, Zhonghua Book Company, 2003, P. 247

19 Qiu Zhao'ao [Qing Dynasty]: *Collected Works of Du Shaoling Annotated*, Vol. 23, Zhonghua Book Company, 1979, P. 2060

20 *The Analects With Notes and Commentary*, Vol.6, *Commentary on the Thirteen Classics*, World Bookstore photocopy of the Ruan woodblock print, P. 2467

21 Liu Yiqing [Song Dynasty of the Southern Dynasties Period]: *New Words for the World* Shanghai Ancient Books Publishing House, 1982

22 Cao Xueqin and Gao E [Qing Dynasty]: *A Dream of Red Mansions* Chapter 44: "Xifeng, Taken by Surprise, Gives Way to Jealousy. Pinger, Unexpectedly Gratified, Makes Her Toilet", People's Literature Publishing House, 1982, P. 613

23 Shi Nai'an [Ming Dynasty]: *Outlaws of the Marsh* Chapter 14: "The Drunken 'Red-Haired Devil' Falls Asleep in Lingguang Temple. 'Heavenly King' Chao Gai Receives His Righteous Followers in Dongxi Village", People's Literature Publishing House, 1975, P. 177

24 Wei Xiuren [Qing Dynasty]: *Traces of the Flowery Moon*, People's Literature Publishing House, 1982, P. 84

25 Cao Xueqin and Gao E [Qing Dynasty]: *A Dream of Red Mansions* Chapter 78: "An Old Scholar at Leisure Has Eulogies Composed. His Unorthodox, Witless Son Laments the Hibiscus", People's Literature Publishing House, 1982, P. 1116

26 Wu Cheng'en [Ming Dynasty]: *Journey to the West* Chapter 38: "The Son Learns From His Mother the Truth of His Usurper Royal Father. The Monkey King Brings the Real Monarch Back to Life With Laojun's Magic Pill." People's Literature Publishing House, 1955, P. 488

27 Guan Hanqing [Yuan Dynasty]: "Bao Zheng Investigates the Case of 'The Butterfly Dream' Three Times", Second Act, *Selected Yuan Dramas*, Zhonghua Book Company, 1958, P. 639

28 Cao Xueqin and Gao E [Qing Dynasty]: *A Dream of Red Mansions* Chapter 7: "Jia Lian Molests Wang Xifeng as He Delivers the Flowers From the Royal Court. Jia Baoyu Runs into Qin Zhong at the Banquet in the Ning Mansion." People's Literature Publishing House, 1982, P. 115

29 Shi Nai'an [Ming Dynasty]: *Outlaws of the Marsh* Chapter 3: "Shi Jin Runs Away From Huayin County at Night. Lu Zhishen Beats Up Zhen Guanxi With His Fists", *Collection of Critiques of Outlaws of the Marsh*, Peking University Press, 1981, P. 93

20 The artistic mood

Artistic mood is formed by a fusion of the creator's subjective feelings and the reflection of objective things in a way that enables the reader to enter deeply into the writer's conceptual world. All the literary genres, such as *shi*, *fu* and *ci* poetry, drama, novels and parallel prose, painting, music – in fact all kinds of art – are created from an artistic mood. Creation which emphasizes artistic mood is a common characteristic of all Chinese art.

The formation of artistic mood, which relies on a fusion of the writer's subjective feelings and the reflection of objective things, comes about either by feelings changing with concrete circumstances, feelings projected onto reality or the closest attention to the way things are. Sometimes the artistic mood can quickly leap to a fresh new stage, and sometimes it needs to begin by deepening the realistic base and preparing the ground for its sublimation. In *Random Poetic Notes of an Old Man* we find: "In Du Fu's 'Toasting the Qu River' there are two verses which were originally as follows: 'The peach blossoms want to converse with the poplar blossoms/From time to time the yellow bird flies with the white bird.' These were changed to 'The peach blossoms want to converse with the poplar blossoms/ From time to time the yellow bird flies with the white bird.'"[1] The change of a mere three words brought about a big change in the artistic mood. Du Fu wrote this poem in the Tang capital of Chang'an in 758, during the reign of Emperor Suzong, from whom he had expected preferment but was disappointed. For a long time he sat on a riverbank, silent and overcome with feelings of loneliness. He felt that the line "The peach blossoms want to converse with the poplar blossoms" was somewhat too lively and did not reflect his present mood, so he changed it to "The peach blossoms want to condole with the poplar blossoms," which better represented his dejected and silent mood of that time.

The artistic mood in *shi* and *ci* poems is particularly fresh and inspirational. Examples are: "Straining my ears I listen but hear nothing all around; I look intensely but see only the white veil of snow" (Tao Yuanming's "A Poem to Cousin Jingyuan in the Mid-Twelfth Chinese Month of the 43rd of the First Thousandth Year, which was 403 CE"); "In a boundless desert lonely smoke rises straight up; Over the endless river the round sun sinks" ("On Mission to the Frontier" by Wang Wei); "Water flows from earth to sky; Hills now appear, now disappear" ("A View of the River Han" by Wang Wei); "A strong wind sprang up and blew away my heart, sending it to Xianyang, where it was caught in a tree" (Li Bai's "Seeing off Wei Ba Who Leaves Rural Jin for the Capital"); "The setting sun shines upon the army flags, the horses neigh in the chilly wind" (Du Fu's "The Second of the Poems Subsequent to the Ones in the 'Crossing the Strategic Pass' Category"); "The boundless crop of autumn leaves/Are rustling ceaselessly down/The endless streams of the Long River/Are rolling forever on" (Du Fu's "Ascending a Height"); "Ran-swollen spring tide rushes by as evening falls/A deserted boat lies by the rustic ferry" (Wei Yingwu's "Mountain Stream West of Chuzhou"); "The sun sets in the west wind/Shining upon the Tomb of Han" (Anonymous, "Yiqin'e (In Memory of a Qin Beauty)"); "A wind springs up abruptly/Wrinkling the water of a spring lake" (Feng Yansi, "Yejinmen (A Visit to the Golden Gate)"); "The moon climbs up and hangs on a willow tree, A young man and woman rendezvous after dusk." (Ouyang Xiu, "Shengzhazi * The First Eve"); "In the setting sun/A few crows scatter; A stream flows by this remote village" (Qin Guan, "Mantingfang (A Courtyard Filled with Flowers)"); "A spring rain spattered the attic all the night, keeping me awake; I heard that apricot blossoms were being peddled in the alley the next morning"; (Lu You, "Just Clearing up after Spring Rain in Lin'an"). It is only by savoring these poetic lines several times over that we can enter upon their artistic mood and enjoy their true beauty.

There are some lyrical essays in praise of scenery and some parallel prose works which also have the artistic mood of poetry. For instance, Wang Bo's "Preface to the Teng Wang Pavilion," Liu Zongyuan's "Eight Records of Yongzhou" and the first and last parts of the "Verses on the Red Cliff" by Su Shi. We can also find this even in prose works by the pre-Qin philosophers. In the "Those of Former Eras" chapter of the *Analects* the disciples Zi Lu, Zeng Xi, Ran You and Gong Xihua are in attendance on Confucius. Their master asks each in turn to speak of his ambition. All except Zeng Xi speak in a straightforward manner. Zeng Xi, however, used highly descriptive language to express his ambition: "In this, the last month of spring, with the dress of the season all complete, along with five or six young men who have assumed the cap, and six or seven boys, I would wash in the Yi, enjoy the breeze among the rain altars, and return home singing."[2] There is artistic mood in this passage.

Is there artistic mood in dramatic works? There is. Wang Guowei, when discussing the subtleties of the poetic drama of the Yuan Dynasty, says, "With one word, the sun is blotted out: This is artistic mood indeed. Why is this called artistic mood? Because when emotions are written about, they sink into the heart; when scenery is written about, it appears to the eye and the ear; when events are written about, it is as if they enunciate themselves."[3] Artistic mood is particularly stressed in the arias of the plays. Some of these arias give a superb depiction of scenery, together with the appropriate atmosphere and the internal stirrings of the personages involved. As such, they are rich in poetic imagery. We can cite the two lines of song from "Parting at the Long Pavilion" from Wang Shifu's *The Western Chamber*:

[Empress] [Duanzhenghao] Clouds in the azure sky, the earth yellow with flowers. The west wind blows hard, the geese fly north to south. Whom do

I see coming entranced from the frost-tinged forest? Always the tears of parting.

[Winding up] On all sides mountain scenes, with only a sliver of light. Worries fill all the people's hearts. How could these carts large and small, many as they are, carry all these cares?[4]

Do novels have artistic mood? Yes, they do too. For instance, the "Green-Robed Girl" in *Strange Tales from a Chinese Studio* relates how a scholar was reading in Jingzai Shrine. In the night he heard a girl cry in admiration from outside the window: "Oh sir, how diligently you study!" Before the young man had time to recover from his amazement, the girl pushed open the door, and, smiling, entered. She was wearing a long green-colored gown and was unutterably charming. The young man fell in love with her immediately, and they spent the night together, during which time he discovered that the girl had a waist which was not enough to fill the grasp of both his hands. She was musically very talented, with a voice that sent the young scholar into raptures. One evening, when the girl had gone to the back of the shrine, the young man heard her calling for help. He discovered that the noise was coming from under the eaves, where a big spider had caught something. It was its prey that was uttering the plaintive cries. The scholar ripped down the spider's web, and rescued the victim, which turned out to be a green bee, on the brink of death. The young man took it back inside with him, and laid it on the table. After a while, the bee seemed to recover. With slow steps it climbed up onto an ink slab and immersed itself in a pool of ink. Crawling back to the table, it wrote upon it the words "Thank you." It then spread its wings and flew out through the window, and was gone forever. The whole of this short story is full of poetic flavor, the final part especially redolent of an artistic mood.

As Chinese literary creation emphasizes artistic mood, so must literary appreciation strive to perceive and enter this artistic mood. When we read works with a profound artistic mood we must completely put aside our surroundings. We see them but don't look at them; we hear them but don't listen to them. Our whole souls must be absorbed in a world of imagination. Sometimes one of our own beautiful experiences is conjured up and chimes with what a poet is saying about something; sometimes, we gain a new understanding of life, of human behavior, of the connection between the universe and humans; sometimes we can transcend our old selves and the limited nature of humans and their knowledge and progress toward a world of more brilliant wisdom.

How then can we enter the artistic mood of a work of literature? It is necessary to give free rein to one's imagination and mental power of association and examine every aspect, going from the surface to deep within. It is not necessary here to go into the function of the imagination and mental power of association in the appreciation of poetry and ballads; the appreciation of traditional opera is all that is needed.

The performance of Chinese opera has a strongly suppositional character. Riding in a carriage, rowing a boat, riding a horse, fighting a battle, knocking at a door, mounting stairs: These are all represented by actors in a highly stylized manner, without the use of stage props. Mountains, rivers, amassed men and horses all spring up in the imagination of the audience. Moreover, the reader of an opera script has no stage directions or indications of scenery or dramatis personae to help him/her. There is just the bare text on the page. But if the reader can use these words to conjure up the various scenes on the stage in his imagination, he can make the dead words come alive and transform themselves into a truly moving spectacle.

Notes

1 Hu Zi [Song Dynasty]: quoted from Vol. 8 of the first part of the collection titled, *Series of Poetic Notes by Fisherman Recluse of the Tiao River*, People's Literature Publishing House, 1962, P. 49
2 *The Analects With Notes and Commentary*, Vol. 11, *Commentary on the Thirteen Classics*, World Bookstore photocopy of the Ruan woodblock print, P. 2500
3 (A Discussion of Song and Yuan Drama)
4 *The Western Chamber*, Chapter 4, People's Literature Publishing House, 1994, PP. 188, 192

21 Focus

Zhong Rong, in his *Poetical Works*, commented on Ruan Ji's poem "Chanted from the Heart" like this: "Describing what I immediately see and hear, I express my feelings about what I perceive in things in the world. The single character used here, meaning to 'lodge' or 'send into,' is close to the two characters 'ji tuo' used by later critics to mean 'focus.' But they are not identical." Later critics also use "xing ji," which is similar to "ji tuo"; for instance, Chen Zi'ang says in his "A Preface to My 'Tall Bamboo' Poem Given to Lieutenant General Dongfang Qiu": "In my leisure time, I often review the poems of the Qi and Liang eras, but I have found them competing in flowery and overloaded language. Each time I lament over their absence of emotional expression through the depiction of objects." His use of "xing ji" here is close to that of "ji tuo." Clearly, these phrases meaning "lodge" or "focus" are a way of representing literary or artistic creation. Wang Shizhen, in his critique titled, "Lovers Sighing over a Flowery Picture," in Volume 11 of his *Literary Notes of Xiang Zu*, says, "The above are four poems by Pan Chun, Zhang Yu, Ni Zan and Xian Wei, respectively. Xian Wei's poem runs as follows:

> The courtyard is empty when spring is late,
> A flower-pitying heart is aged by the wind.
> I know that favor won't fall on ill-fated me,
> So I desire no money to buy expensive poems.

This is an example of focus.

Focus is of course a way of veiling a meaning, but it often does this by use of romantic images, and the meaning tends to be biased toward an appeal to the governing powers or the expression of a political grievance, or it could hint at the moral character or personality of the writer. In this respect, the general meaning and the hidden meaning of a work are often at odds. Chinese literature has a figurative tradition. The "The Master Shunned" chapter of the *Analects* says, "When the year becomes cold, then we know how the pine and the cypress are the last to lose their leaves."[1] In this case, the pine and cypress are images borrowed to represent a staunch and upright character. In the "Li Sao," the romantic image of "beautiful women and fragrant grass" is borrowed to represent the lofty mind and moral integrity of the poet. Some writers do not dare or are unwilling to express their political views openly and so use figurative language to express them. Some such works are those titled, "Chanted from the Heart," "Singing of History," "Disappointment" and "Recalling with Emotion." Therefore, to appreciate Chinese literature the first thing to do is decide whether a particular work has "focus" or not. If it has, then the next step is to identify that "focus" and grasp the author's true meaning and emotion by penetrating the surface images. Take, for instance the second part of Li Shangyin's "Seeing a Rain-Battered Peony on the Way Home":

> Laugh not at the pomegranate flowers budding after spring,
> The peony flowers fallen before summer are more saddening.
> Rain drops beating on the petals like tears dropping on a plate,
> Wind awakens me from my dreams like zithers of fifty strings.
> Enshrouded in a foggy haze, the garden is no longer what it was,
> Lives exuberant all year round are reduced to drifting dust.
> The peonies looking back at me in Qianxi like dainty dancers,
> Now thinking of you, I find novelty in your graceful blooms.[2]

In this poem the rain-battered peony is a metaphor for the poet himself. The description of an object and the expression of emotion are mingled, and both tortuous and simple approaches are utilized to describe the misfortunes he has encountered. Another example is found in "White Plum" by the Yuan Dynasty poet Wang Mian:

> My body freezes in the snowy forest,
> The different odors of peach and plum,
> mingle with the scent of the earth.
> Suddenly in the night a clear scent,
> Pervades the whole universe.[3]

Under the poet's brush the white plum tree emerges as noble and pure. Moreover, it does not enjoy its perfume all by itself; it wishes to share it, in order to hasten the advent of spring. This is an example of the focusing of the poet's imagination.

Not a few works employing the technique of focus are found among prose writings. In the fourth part of Han Yu's *Miscellaneous Discourses*, the author uses the metaphor of the mythical "Thousand-Li Horse" (the Chinese Pegasus) to represent the universal sufferings of the poor scholar:

> It was only after the horse-master Bo Le appeared on earth that the thousand-li horse did too. After that, there were many such horses, but only one Bo Le. There were many famous horses, but they were ashamed to be under the control of slaves, and died in droves between the manger and the stable, and were never recognized as thousand-li horses. A thousand-li horse could eat a trough-full of fodder at a time. Those who ate horse flesh did not know

they were eating that of thousand-li horses. Such a horse, although it had the ability to gallop for one thousand li, was never fed enough and never had sufficient strength, and so its beauty was never appreciated. Because it could not be compared to ordinary horses, how could it be recognized as a thousand-li horse? It could not be brought to answer to the whip, nor could it be fed enough to be able to display its talents to the full. It would not obey the commands of its master, who would face it with the whip, and sigh, "There are no decent horses any more!" Alas, is it true that there are no longer any decent horses? Or is it just that truly outstanding horses are not recognized?[4]

In his "Words of Admiration for the Lotus," Zhou Dunyi of the Song Dynasty uses the metaphor of the lotus emerging unsullied from the slime to describe his own integrity. This is another famous example of focus in a literary work.

Nevertheless, in literary appreciation we must avoid forced analogies, which may make us see "focus" in works where in fact there is none. This will drain all interest from appreciation of a literary work and be a stumbling block in the way of understanding it. The Confucianists of the Han Dynasty often made this mistake with regard to the *Book of Odes*. For instance, the "Osprey" is clearly a love song, but it was interpreted as "the virtue of a secondary wife." Chen Chen of the Qing Dynasty followed the Han Confucianists' method of interpreting the *Book of Odes*, and as a consequence made a number of false analogies. An example of this is the Han Dynasty Music Bureau's interpretation of the "Shang Ye": "Shang Ye! I want to be your confidant always. Without a lapse throughout life. When the mountains prove no barrier and the river's waters flow unceasing, when thunder rumbles in winter, and rain and snow fall in summer, when Heaven and Earth come together, then and only then will I be parted from my lord."[5]

Chen Chen says, "Isn't this a *ci* poem about a loyal official protesting against calumny?"[6] Clearly it is a satire on corruption.

Notes

1 *The Analects With Notes and Commentary, Commentary on the Thirteen Classics*, World Bookstore photocopy of the Ruan woodblock print, P. 2491
2 Feng Hao [Qing Dynasty]: *Collected Poems of Yu Xisheng With Commentary and Notes*, Vol. 1, Shanghai Ancient Books Publishing House, 1979, P. 117
3 Wang Wan [Yuan Dynasty]: *Collected Poems From the Bamboo Studio*, Vol. 4, *Collected Works of Mr. Shao Wuxu*
4 Ma Tongbo: *Collected Works of Han Changli Collated With Notes*, Vol. 1, Classical Literature Publishing House, 1957, P. 20
5 Guo Maoqing [Song Dynasty]: *Collected Poems of the Music Bureau*, Vol. 16, Zhonghua Book Company, 1979, P. 231
6 Chen Shen [Qing Dynasty]: *A Letter About the Explicit and Implied Comparisons in Poetry*, Vol. 1, Shanghai Ancient Books Publishing House, 1981, P. 14

22 Extensive gathering of knowledge

The appreciation of Chinese literature requires a widespread and solid grounding in Chinese culture. For instance, in the appreciation of poetry and ballads there are many parallels with the artistic theories of painting and calligraphy. Wang Yuanqi of the Qing Dynasty, when commenting on landscape painting, says that the use of the brush means the use of "hair" (the major part of the character for "brush"), and Cai Yong, when discussing the art of calligraphy, stresses "abstruseness." These two comments correspond to the use of the terms "application" and "clumsiness" used by the critics when discussing the art of poetry and balladry. Thus the two approaches confirm each other. Discussing the poems of Han Wei in his *The Origin of Poetry*, Ye Xie says, "His application to his art lies in his clumsiness, and his clumsiness lies in his application to his art."[1] Chen Shidao, discussing a poem by Liu Yuxi, in his *Talks on the Poems of Hou Shan*, says, "His words are clumsy, but they make clear his application to his art."[2] In his *Talks on the Poems of Sui Yuan*, Yuan Mei says, "Poems should be straightforward, not ingeniously worded, and then do they display the simplicity of great ingenuity; poems should be plain and not deep, and then do they display the plainness of depth."[3] There is an identical thread linking what the painter calls "hair," what the calligrapher calls "abstruseness" and what the poet calls "clumsiness."

Traditional Chinese art puts a lot of emphasis on the word "empty," and postulates that wherever there is "emptiness" there is actuality. A painter will often leave a large blank space in a painting, allowing the viewer to use his/her imagination to fill it up. Da Zhongguang, a painter of the early Qing Dynasty, says in his "Painting a Fish Trap": "Emptiness and actuality give birth to one another. In no painting is every spot a fine scene."[4] Calligraphers and seal carvers have a saying: "Calligraphy and painting are so far apart that a horse can gallop between them, and yet are so near that even a gust of wind cannot pass between them. Fascination emerges when white can present itself as black." The pursuit of "the meaning outside the words" of Chinese literature is exactly the same in essence as the "actuality in the emptiness" and "white presenting itself as black"; the reader sees words where there are none, and thereby grasps the real meaning of the work. If one can comprehend the art of Chinese painting, calligraphy and seal carving, this is a help toward appreciating Chinese literature.

A knowledge of foreign literatures is also necessary for a complete apprecia-tion of Chinese literature, from the angle of comparison. Whether the compari-son is between works of the same genre, works with the same theme or works of the same epoch, it is always useful for literary appreciation. On the subject of the comparison and appreciation of foreign literature vis-à-vis Chinese lit-erature, Mr. Qian Zhongshu's *Records of Discussions of Art* and *Compositions by Guan Zhui* are successful examples of this, and no more need be said about them. Mr. Nagashima has compared *A Garden of Tang Poems* by Zhang Zhixiang of the Ming Dynasty with the volumes of Japanese poems titled, *Collection of Eight Generations* and *Collection of Thirteen Generations*. The Chinese poems are lined up under the headings Spring, Autumn, Summer and Winter, while the Japanese poems are arranged under the headings Autumn, Spring, Winter and Summer. The majority of the former are grouped under the heading Spring, and the latter under Autumn, and from this we can get a glimpse of the difference in literary psychology between the two countries.[5]

Notes

1 Ye Xie [Qing Dynasty]: *The Origin of Poetry*, second part of the unofficial edition, People's Literature Publishing House, 1979, P. 62
2 He Wenhuan ed. [Qing Dynasty]: *Notes on Poems Through the Ages*, Zhonghua Book Company, 1981, P. 302
3 Yuan Mei [Qing Dynasty]: *Talks on the Poetry of Sui Yuan*, Vol. 5, People's Literature Publishing House, 1982, P. 150
4 Da Zhongguang [Qing Dynasty]: "Painting a Fish Trap", *Collected Works From Lack of Knowledge Studio*, Vol. 12, woodblock print, sixth year (1826) of the Daoguang reign period of the Qing Dynasty
5 Nakashima (Japan): *A Study of the Garden of Tang Poems*, Kyuko Shoin, 1995

Interim summary

To sum up, I want to discuss two points:

First, I attempted to establish a viewpoint on the "position of literature" in the "General Summary" of my *History of Chinese Literature* (of four volumes).[1] The general idea is this: To treat literature as a subject of study it is necessary to concentrate on the special points that give it its artistic influence and esthetic value. The "position of literature" cannot be divorced from textual criticism, study of its social background, etc. This is very important indeed, for otherwise the study of literature would not have a firm basis. Each literary researcher has an individual specialty, and there is no hierarchy in this field. Of course, in literary research literary works are the core. But there are two more levels of attention: One is the creators of literature themselves, and the other is the social background to the works and their creators. Whichever level is concentrated on, it will revolve around the actual works of literature, because all such efforts are aimed at expounding on and clarifying those works. Also in my "General Summary" I discuss "historical trends of thought" and the "cultural point of view" and their connection with the "position of literature." These two approaches are important in that they complement and enrich each other, affording a wide perspective on the "position of literature."

Second, literature comprises a world of its own created by mankind outside the objective world. This is a spiritual world, or it could be called an illusory and yet real world. It is an incomparably rich and lively world. It unfolds a world of boundless imagination. Faced with the task of explaining this world, the literary researcher must be equipped to a high degree with a number of skills: reasoning ability, the ability to handle documents, a wide range of general knowledge and artistic sensitivity, appreciation and creativity. The importance of the last three is worth stressing. Moreover, the cultivation of these qualities is never-ending. It is not that waiting until one's qualities have reached a certain level that one can then engage in literary research, but that in the course of such research one's own qualities are gradually raised.

Note

1 Yuan Xingpei (chief ed.): *History of Chinese Literature*, Vol. 1, Higher Education Press, P. 3

Afterword to the first Chinese edition

The manuscript of this book was submitted to the Hong Kong branch of the San-lian Bookshop in October last year (1987), and at the beginning of this year (1988) the copyright was sold by Sanlian Bookshop to Taiwan Wu-Nan Book Company Ltd. In September 1988 the book was published in Taiwan, and a Hong Kong edition was expected shortly. It is reported that the book, not long after publication, was chosen as a textbook by several universities in Taiwan. A Japanese-language edition is planned. This has all been very gratifying to the author, but even more pleasing is the kind agreement of the Higher Education Press to make the book available to the general reader.

Looking back at when I first took up the task, I remember that I was far from confident that I could accomplish it. Keeping in mind the fact that no such book as this had been written in the previous 40 years, I could only rely on my own meager understanding of the subject as I strove to forge a systematic *Outline*. The *Outline* I came up with was different from the standard histories and introductions to Chinese literature, as it was to encompass every aspect and the complete course of development of Chinese literature. Also, it had to explain in clear and concise language the theoretical aspects of the subject. It was difficult indeed to complete such a task equipped with only my own limited knowledge. In the course of writing this book I had to keep reminding myself that I was to write from an individual perspective, marked by individual characteristics; I was not setting out to write a general introduction to Chinese literature. And this only added to the difficulties. Now, when I presume to glance over this book with the eye of the general reader I can't avoid feeling a sort of inexpressible regret. However, I do not feel any compulsion to embark on a hasty revision, as only 14 months has passed since the manuscript left my hands, and no revision at this stage would lead to any great improvement. It would perhaps be better to wait until later for revision.

Here the author would like to tender his warmhearted thanks to all the scholars in both China and Japan who have shown interest in this book from the time of writing to its publication, as well as to all the people of publishing circles for their support!

Yuan Xingpei
November 3, 1988

Afterword to the second Chinese edition

In 1987 I was invited to invited to lecture on Chinese literature at Japan's Aichi University. Not long afterwards my lecture notes were published separately by Hong Kong's Sanlian Bookshop, Taiwan Wu-Nan Book Company Ltd. and the mainland's Higher Education Press.

This book has been warmly received by a large number of readers, not only on China's mainland, but in Hong Kong and Taiwan too. It has also been chosen as a textbook for use in several high schools. Last year the Higher Education Press expressed the hope that I would arrange for a revised and enlarged edition of the book. I thought that this was a good suggestion, and I have now finished working on this second edition. I have kept the original format and framework and the points of view which pervade the text, but I have readjusted some of the sections, fleshed out many of the contents and improved the wording in not a few places. Since the first edition came out there has been a great development in the study of Chinese literature, and many of the problems raised in the first edition – such as those of the territorial background to Chinese literature, its types, the evolution of literary works and the characteristics of style, the interactions between different types of writing and some of the rules dictating the course of development of Chinese literature – have all received attention to various degrees from the academic community. Moreover, I have taken the opportunity of this second edition to add a chapter titled, "The Methods and Media of the Transmission of Chinese Literature" to tentatively explore a question which I neglected in the first edition and which still has not been fully studied by scholars.

There is one more point which I should bring to the attention of the readers: This book was written from a highly individualistic point of view. Based on my own appreciation as a reader of the works of ancient literature, I have striven to express in simple language the depth of my various related impressions, especially to convey the aspects of such writings that moved me, in the hope that the readers can share my emotions. Since this book is an "outline" of Chinese literature it covers literary works and the aspects of literature that move people, as well as the aesthetic values therein. And because it is an "outline" it is not meant to be, nor is there any need for it to be exhaustive. Moreover, it is not overloaded with discussions; many of the points of view are the author's own. I have concentrated on piquing the reader's curiosity, and this endeavor too is in itself a form of academic pursuit.

In the Afterword to the first edition I expressed my thanks to both scholars and people of publishing circles involved in the work. Since its publication I have received many messages of encouragement from readers, and Mr. Luo Zongqiang and Mr. Lin Donghai have been kind enough to write positive reviews. Not long ago, I happened to read a book review by a scholar I am unacquainted with which recommended my book, and he later sent me a very encouraging letter. I heartily thank Mr. Cheng Qianfan. Generally speaking, personal letters usually contain no more than polite clichés, but Mr Cheng's "The *Outline* is no ordinary work. In fact, it probes into the very marrow of its subjects. Eminent scholars will agree with me" (see *Correspondence from the Leisurely Hall*), I am convinced, is no mere lip service. It has been scholars of the senior and present generations and the general body of readers who have given me the confidence to expand and revise this work which I completed over 10 years ago. I wish to take this opportunity to express once more my sincere gratitude to them all!

Back in 1987, when I wrote the manuscript for this book, I used to rise at 4 a.m. every day, and work on it for over 10 hours. I would churn out the pages on an old mimeograph machine and number the rough drafts with a pencil. Then I would ask my students to help me to check each page. I had plenty of energy in those days, and as I considered this task a worthwhile use of my time I completed the book from start to finish at one go. From 1987 to now 18 years have passed, and I too have passed through middle age to old age. That this book is now presented to the readers in a new format is deeply gratifying. I wish to tell them that of all my published writings the process of writing this one was the most pleasant.

Yuan Xingpei
April 18, 2005

Index

For Product Safety Concerns and Information please contact our EU
representative GPSR@taylorandfrancis.com
Taylor & Francis Verlag GmbH, Kaufingerstraße 24, 80331 München, Germany